THE POLITICS OF PRIVACY

THE POLITICS OF PRIVACY

Planning for Personal Data Systems as Powerful Technologies

James Rule
Douglas McAdam
Linda Stearns
David Uglow

Elsevier • New York
New York • Oxford

To the memory of
George Orwell

Exclusive Distribution throughout the World by Greenwood Press, Westport, Ct. U.S.A.

Elsevier North Holland, Inc.
52 Vanderbilt Avenue, New York, New York 10017

Published by arrangement with
The New American Library, Inc., New York, New York.

Library of Congress Cataloging in Publication Data

Main entry under title:

The Politics of privacy.

Bibliography: p.
Includes index.
1. Privacy, Right of—United States. 2. Computers—Access control.
I. Rule, James.
JC596.2.U5P64 323.44'83'0973 80-13788
ISBN 0-444-99074-7

Manufactured in the United States of America

Contents

Preface

Some ten years ago James Rule began to be fascinated by the growing importance of personal documentation—files, certificates, credit cards, dossiers, and the like—in modern, highly "developed" societies. At the time, most people seemed to find this a perverse academic interest. It was neither a standard subject for sociological research nor a well-defined topical social issue.

Rule's researches eventually led to publication, in 1973, of *Private Lives and Public Surveillance.* By then, no special explanation for interest in bureaucratic uses of personal information was required. Public controversy over such matters had built considerably, and a number of scholarly and popular writings had appeared to deal with the issue. Rule's book took its place as one of a number of studies on what came to be known as "the privacy issue."

In a sense, this book is a sequel to *Private Lives and Public Surveillance.* The earlier book analyzed the uses of personal-data systems in five government and private organizations in Britain and America. Since consciousness of "the privacy issue" was just taking shape as it was being written, *Private Lives and Public Surveillance* did not have a great deal to say on the public controversies themselves. By now, however, sensitivity to the issue is acute, and an official line of "privacy policy" has taken shape both in America and abroad. This book offers an analysis and critique of that policy response.

The beginning of this book came with an invitation to James Rule in 1976 from the Federal Privacy Protection Study Commission to prepare a report for the commission staff. That report was to review the development of the privacy issue in sociological perspective, and to comment on the emerging policy responses to these trends. Writing this report provided a happy opportunity to exchange views with those actually charged with recommending legislation and policy. Indeed, the experience was so stimulating that it became impossible to leave the project alone, once the report was completed early in 1977. Rule therefore approached the other three authors in the fall of that year, and sought their cooperation in developing a book out of the earlier work. The four were already associated in a National Science Foundation sponsored study relating to privacy; agreeing to extend the ongoing collaboration to include work on this book thus seemed easy and natural.

The writing of this book took place between December 1977 and January 1979. Building on the Rule report to the Privacy Commission, the authors have developed additional information to extend and buttress its arguments. As drafts of the book have emerged, all four authors have argued over them, suggesting improvements for future versions, and have assembled further amplifying material. Thus the four take full responsibility for the facts and viewpoints put forward here; they are collective products, reached through thorough and often contentious discussion of the points involved.

Thanks are owing to a great many institutions and persons for their help in creating this book. We are grateful first of all to the Sociology Department of the State University of New York, Stony Brook, for providing a setting for the work, and to the National Science Foundation, Division of Mathematical and Computer Sciences, for bringing us together as a research team. NSF funds have not provided actual support for the preparation and writing of this book, although a few findings from our NSF study are mentioned here in passing. But the NSF grant did provide the basis for our original collaboration, and thus contributed indirectly to our efforts here.

Further thanks are owing to the John Simon Guggenheim

Memorial Foundation, whose fellowship provided to James Rule the time off from normal academic responsibilities during which this book was written. Rule spent the fellowship year at the Center for Advanced Study in the Behavioral Sciences, that most conducive of all environments to academic pursuits. His work at the Center for Advanced Study was made possible by NSF grant BNS-76-22943. The authors take pleasure in recording their sincere thanks to all these institutions.

Another major debt of thanks is owed to those who served on the staff of the Privacy Protection Study Commission, and especially to Carole Parsons, formerly its executive director, and to Chris Heller. The commission staff provided both the occasion for the first work on these ideas and, later on, the most penetrating yet balanced criticism of the manuscript as it took shape. Given that the commission staff often felt sharp disagreement with views put forward here, their thoughtful and painstaking criticism strikes us as little short of noble.

A number of other well-informed commentators have also reviewed this manuscript at various stages and offered suggestions for its improvement. These include Paul Armer, Kent Greenawalt, Rob Kling, Theodore Lowi, Charles Marson, David B.H. Martin, Charles Perrow, and a number of others. Here, too, we have received much more good advice than we have been able or willing to accept. But we feel that we have profited at least some from all of it.

In developing the material for this book, particular burdens fell on the librarians of the Center for Advanced Study in the Behavioral Sciences, Margaret Amara and Chris Hoth. For their painstaking and thoroughly professional help, the authors offer their deepest thanks.

Finally, the authors are indebted to Heather McLean and a number of other secretaries at the Center for Advanced Study in Stanford, and to Mary Luyster at Stony Brook, for indefatigable clerical help.

It is always a pleasure for writers to record thanks of this kind; for readers, such thanks may offer useful clues to the influences which shape a particular work. The authors do not wish to spread responsibility for the views expressed here, however. We have deliberately chosen to write a controversial book. We take full responsibility for the viewpoints developed here, and we hope that they challenge others to sharpen their positions in turn.

James Rule
Douglas McAdam
Linda Stearns
David Uglow

Introduction

Privacy means many different things. For a homeowner, it may mean a hedge around the backyard to fend off looks from neighbors or passersby. For a celebrity, it may mean the chance to go about in public without being recognized. For lovers, it may mean the chance to say things to be heard only by one another. For a lawyer and client, it may mean the ability to discuss their case with certainty that other parties cannot hear. For a child, it may mean a secret place to play, or just to be alone with one's thoughts. For a job applicant, it may mean not having to discuss certain periods of one's past with the prospective employer, or not disclosing one's minimum salary requirements.

Many languages have no single term with all the implications of our "privacy." The fact that the term is so rich makes generalizations about privacy tenuous. Perhaps the only safe generalization is that the status of privacy in the modern world is changing. The possibilities of enjoying privacy, in virtually every sense of the term, are not what they have been nor, apparently, what they are going to be. Changes central to the workings of modern societies seem to be affecting privacy in all of its forms.

In the last fifteen years, many of these changes have become politicized. People have begun to think of privacy as an endangered value, as something to be protected through public action. Thus national politics in America have produced a Privacy Act, a Privacy Protection Study Commission, suggestions for a permanent Privacy Board, and a variety of similar measures suggested or contemplated. But these controversies have not involved privacy in all of its many senses. Instead, they have centered on privacy issues associated with the bureaucratic use of dossiers, computer files, and other personal data systems. It is the growth of such systems which has spurred the emergence of "the privacy issue," as people know it nowadays.

The rise of the issue obviously reflects profound changes in the social structuring of personal data. Once, the details of most people's lives were strictly local concerns. The facts of one's birth, the circumstances of one's upbringing, the skills or training one acquired, one's choice of mate or means of livelihood, and, ultimately, one's demise were known only to a handful of intimates. True, a few "great men" might gain regional or even wider repute, and the details of their lives thus spread. But most people's reputations, most of the time, were narrowly known. Like that of a pebble dropped into a small pond, the report of a single life did not carry very far.

So things went in what sociologists call traditional societies. With the growth of the modern state, however, things began to change, and since the turn of the twentieth century, in the most "developed" societies, these changes have plunged ahead precipitately. People now move about more, but this is hardly the main thing. For the facts of people's biographies circulate whether they themselves do or not. Even the most obscure and least mobile members of modern societies have the details of their lives recorded and stored in distant places by distant agencies. More remarkable still, the substance and uses of these records *matter* to the people concerned to an extent that would have astounded our grandparents. For the written records of one's life, in modern America and other developed countries, shape the treatments one receives by organizations. And the role of organizations, both private and public, is powerful indeed.

Indeed, our expectations of organizations help perpetuate and extend their record-keeping bent. We expect, even demand, that distant agencies, from the Social Security Administration to credit-card firms, deal with us "personally." That is, we expect such organizations to take full account of our unique needs, backgrounds, qualifications, and special circumstances. We assume as much about the agencies which assess tax liabilities, determine insurance rates, issue driving licenses, or process security clearances. And organizations can only fulfill these expectations through documentary record-keeping on the people concerned. Thus these bodies may come to rival the importance in traditional settings of neighbors, family, and other face-to-face intimates in their effects on our lives. And in thoroughness, the cold intimacy of their bureaucratic attentions may rival the intrusive nosiness of the small town or extended family.

Most Americans have long known that present-day organizations maintain vast personal-data files. Yet it is worth reviewing briefly the size and scope of some of the most impressive of these.

The system with perhaps the most comprehensive documentary coverage of the adult population is the Internal Revenue Service. This system assembles a rich array of pertinent data on at least 85 million individuals and married couples. The files are increasingly computerized, to facilitate inquiries from outlying IRS offices to central data banks.

Scarcely less impressive in these respects, however, are the wholly nongovernmental files maintained by the credit-reporting industry. Data held in these files deal with such things as place of work and residence, income, marital status and history, assets and financial obligations, and credit use; reports based on such information are sold to credit grantors for use in evaluating credit applications from consumers. The increasingly computerized credit-reporting industry is estimated to have some 150 million credit histories in file as of 1977. Bureaus in America probably sell over 130 million reports per year.

Nearly matching this level of activity among governmental record systems are the systems maintained by the FBI. Here there are many distinct files. The largest of these is the fingerprint file, with some 60 million sets of prints. Other FBI files include those of the computerized National Crime Information Center, which supplies state and local law-enforcement agencies with data on crimes and criminals. The FBI claims that this system embodies some 6 million different items of data, ranging from information on stolen property to complete criminal history records.

To these mammoth systems we could add many others, including record systems maintained by Social Security, the CIA, insurance companies, credit-card firms, state and local law-enforcement agencies, the security-clearance system, and many others. All of these systems embody entries on literally millions of persons. In addition, many smaller repositories of information, though individually less impressive, account in aggregate for further millions of files. And let us make no mistake—all of these systems affect the interests of those portrayed in them. Were they not indispensable for organizational decision-making, they would not warrant the enormous expense required for their creation and maintenance.

But although the existence of these systems is generally recognized, the varied and sophisticated *uses* of their data would surprise most people. The IRS, for example, has developed a computerized technique for scanning all returns in search of what officials call "audit potential." A statistical rating system flags those returns showing similarities to returns found delinquent in the past. The ability thus to select a minority of "suspect" returns from the otherwise unmanageable total provides a key advantage in enforcement.

Or consider the resourcefulness of credit-card systems in monitoring the use of their cards. VISA, for example, maintains an up-to-the-minute computerized record of the status of each account, including the maximum credit allowed, the amount of debt outstanding, and the timing and nature of recent purchases. This computerized data bank also contains other pertinent data on the card holder and the card itself—including whether it has been reported missing. Charges above a certain limit on the VISA card must be cleared by telephone with VISA headquarters. There the staff assess the requested charges in light of the whole record. They can and do decline those charges which seem to exceed the ability of the card holder to pay. And when the system registers an attempt to use a card reported stolen, it may dispatch the police to arrest the would-be user before he or she can leave the store.

Indeed, consumer credit has produced some of the most remarkable innovations in resourceful uses of data files. Some credit bureaus invite credit grantors to subscribe to a "watch list," an early-warning system on consumer delinquencies. For a fee, the participating businesses are warned when one of their credit customers, in light of all the information available to the bureau, appears in danger of becoming "overloaded" with excessive credit obligations. This enables the creditors to restrict the credit accounts of these persons before they become delinquent.

The effectiveness of many of these techniques stems from the numbers of persons covered by the systems. Under Congressional mandate, for example, the IRS and Social Security Administration in recent years have become involved in the Parent Locator Service, a national system for tracking parents who abscond leaving dependent children on public support. Through the use of records from these and other federal agencies, the Parent Locator Service exposes such persons to legal action to enforce support obligations. Since it is difficult to live in America today without at least occasional communication with the IRS or Social Security, this technique can be very effective.

Such sophisticated uses of personal information have caused most indignation where they have been farthest removed from the uses intended when the data were provided. Many people have been disturbed to find that IRS files, for example, are used by government attorneys for jury selection, to eliminate jurors who might have strong predispositions against the government. But these practices are no doubt less emotionally charged than the *political* uses of IRS files which culminated in the Watergate period. Here the White House targeted both individuals and organizations regarded as political enemies for unfriendly surveillance. In some instances the IRS undertook audits aimed at harassing those concerned; elsewhere, the White House funneled tax-return data to other agencies, including the CIA and FBI, for action against the organizations and persons involved.

The Watergate disclosures brought public concern over organizational uses and misuses of personal data to a boiling point. But clearly those events did no more than to heighten trends already under way. Agencies of all kinds, public and private, were collecting more and more documentary information on people. And people now understood that the data so compiled were being misused in the ways described above. The only thing one could be sure of was that these uses were likely to have far-reaching effects on one's life. The uneasiness over those effects, rising to indignation as particularly outrageous practices came to light, formed the raw material for "the privacy issue." The rise of this issue, and its assimilation in American political life, is the subject of this book.

Public anxieties about large-scale personal record-keeping have been well-founded. Well-founded not in the sense that everyone's most outlandish fears on these subjects have reflected actual record-keeping practices. But well founded in a broader sense of pointing to authentic and enduring issues in modern societies. Documentary information on otherwise obscure and anonymous people now provides a source of strength to organizations of all kinds. These powers of organizational action may serve the most beneficent social purposes, or the most dreadful. They may enable organizations to deliver medical care, or to snoop into the lives of political enemies. Whether any particular use of these systems is desirable or not, their cumulative growth changes something fundamental about the relationship between powerful institutions and their publics. These changes ought well to give us pause.

At some point the powers conferred by maintenance and use of sophisticated personal-data systems must be counted excessive. Where to place that point, however, is a subtle and contentious matter. It turns on concerns which go well beyond characteristics of the data systems themselves; these include the risks of misuse of power in our society, the desirability of holding people responsible for past misdeeds, and the inherent worth of private experience.

These questions cannot be answered, even in principle, on wholly objective grounds. Thus though we have our own strong opinions on these matters, our purpose here is not to argue for any particular "solution" to "the privacy problem." Indeed, we will argue that the nature of the issues at stake defies any unique "solution." But we do insist that public consideration of, and the official response to, these matters has thus far been inadequate. The most compelling questions, we will argue, have been omitted from discussion.

This sleight-of-hand is particularly evident in the fate of the term "privacy" itself in official discussion. In an interview not long after taking office, former FBI director Clarence

Kelley answered questions on that organization's uses of data files. Referring to the National Crime Information Center and its computerized data-sharing potentials, the interviewer asked about dissemination of FBI data on people's criminal histories. Kelley replied,

> They are available to members of the family of law enforcement—the police, the prosecutors, the judiciary, the corrections, parole and probation agencies. And they also can be made available to outsiders for research.

Then, in a remarkable observation, Kelley added, "If this is done properly, it's not a breach of privacy."[1]

One may well argue that the dealing with convicted criminals warrants demands on their privacy which would elsewhere be unacceptable. But to suggest that the manipulations of personal information described above do not infringe privacy deprives the word "privacy" of all meaning. If taken seriously, this way of talking could define privacy out of existence.

Though slightly clumsier than most, Kelley's efforts to avoid a distasteful reality by changing its name typifies the official response to "the privacy issue." There can be no doubt that organizations' personal record-keeping practices infringe on privacy as most people use that term. Whether other social goods which may arise from such record-keeping warrant such infringement is a matter for discussion. But it will not do to suggest that no conflict, and hence no authentic issues for choice, exist.

Nevertheless, most discussions of "the privacy issue" have played down the most important choices: How much personal record-keeping is desirable? How far should the growth of these systems go? When does the use of personal-data files, even for good purposes, become too much of a good thing? In developing programs for "reform" of these systems, the reformers have glossed over these critical questions. Instead, they have concentrated on developing official "rules of the game" to guide operations of personal-data systems. Such rules have typically sought to ensure the accuracy and pertinence of data held in file, to create ways for people to mon-

[1] *U.S. News and World Report,* 15 October 1973, p. 59.

itor and to influence the uses of their own files, and to limit data-management activities to those essential to the efficiency of the data-keeping organizations. If these goals are fulfilled, it is assumed, "privacy" is "protected."

The trouble is, modern organizations are continually developing ingenious and efficient ways of collecting and using more and more personal data. The growing demands for personal information which result from this steady innovation can only result in mounting pressures on privacy. Procedural measures such as those described above do little to countervail against such pressures; indeed, by making personal-data systems more publicly acceptable, these reforms streamline the systems' accelerating growth. And as long as these systems continue to grow, they can only continue to erode individual privacy and autonomy.

Thus the "reform" of personal-data systems, though often desirable, hardly addresses the fundamental social choices posed by the growth of the systems. Despite the fond hopes of the reformers, we cannot really expect to enjoy both more personal-data management and more privacy and freedom. On the contrary, a meaningful approach to the protection of privacy means encouraging organizations to collect and use less information on people, rather than more.

But such an approach requires fundamental change in people's expectations of modern organizations. For, as we noted above, a deepgoing assumption of our times is that organizations must deal with people in light of the precise details of their backgrounds and situations. And such dealings require recourse to data files—to document the facts on which key decisions depend. To suggest minimizing reliance on such files is to strike at a key source of organizational advantage—and at a source of often attractive organizational services.

But alternatives to such reliance can and should be sought. If we are serious about protecting privacy, we ought to demand development of less "information-intensive" alternatives to practices now requiring personal data. We ought to seek ways of administering income taxation, for example, which take into account fewer details of people's lives in assessing tax liability, and thus require fewer personal data. We ought to explore ways of providing consumer credit and insurance which require less inquiry into the backgrounds and characteristics of applicants. We ought to seek alternatives to the demeaning invasions of privacy made against applicants for welfare and other social services—perhaps by minimizing eligibility requirements in favor of a guaranteed floor under all incomes. We ought to cut back on the amount and the kinds of information which employers seek in screening job applicants. All of these and other alternatives to increasing reliance on personal-data systems would threaten the efficiency of powerful bureaucracies. Yet they would by the same token win gains for a looser, more private world.

If such alternatives are not sought, present policies can only foster continued growth in personal-data systems. This will mean a growth in the power of bureaucratic institutions, both public and private, over the lives of those with whom these institutions deal. Thus the growth of a more regulated, more orderly world—but also a less private, more tightly controlled one. Probably no one really desires or prefers to live in such a world; yet the fundamental changes necessary to reverse our drift in this direction are painful to adopt.

The dilemmas posed by these alternatives have much in common with other issues of our times. Modern societies seem to have a special affinity for "big" technologies—ones which, like nuclear-power generation or the control of genetic inheritance, place new and sweeping powers in human hands. Often these new powers promise extraordinary benefits in terms of human comfort and well-being. But they also entail extraordinary risks, should they be misused. Thus a mistake in the working of a nuclear-power plant, or a miscalculation in modern military strategy, may have much graver implications than their counterparts in less sophisticated and powerful systems. When powerful, modern technologies go wrong, they can go wrong in egregiously destructive ways. So it is with personal-data systems. They confer unprecedented power upon bureaucracies to pursue their ends efficiently; but the existence of these powers poses risks which must at some point be counted unacceptable.

How are we to identify that point? How can we develop alternatives to risky reliance on very large, very powerful, and very privacy-invading information systems? And how can planners be encouraged to take seriously the notion that bigger, more powerful systems for monitoring people's lives are not necessarily better? In struggling to answer these questions, we confront the key issues of how to live with all sorts of powerful modern technologies.

PART I

The Emergence of an Issue

Privacy has long been an important concept in Western thinking, but it has not always been a political issue. An issue is something whose present state is unstable or unsatisfactory, something which therefore demands choices for action. In America and other Western societies, privacy has emerged as an issue within the last fifteen years.

People believe that this development is not accidental, but that the emergence of privacy as an issue has something to do with distinctive qualities of the times in which we live. Most people would probably identify technological change in general, and the development of computing in particular, as responsible for this emergence. The new technologies, it is felt, lead people to collect, store, and use all sorts of personal information which previously could not be treated in these ways. And these new treatments of personal data give rise to conflicts which are the making of political issues.

We believe that these views are correct, though only as far as they go. New technologies do indeed make possible many of the treatments of personal information leading to present-day privacy controversies; elsewhere, however, the controversies stem from uses of technologies which have been with us for a long time. The key condition for the emergence of the privacy issue in the 1960s and 1970s, we feel, is not any particular technology so much as new social relationships. The social structures of advanced industrial society give rise to distinctive demands (often but not always abetted by new technologies) for personal information. We need to take a close look at the origins of these demands.

1 □ Some Historical Precedents

Concern over privacy in the 1960s and 1970s has spawned a handful of scholarly studies of the evolution of privacy in American life. One of these is *Privacy in Colonial New England*, by David Flaherty.[1] The picture which Flaherty paints offers a striking mixture of similarities and contrasts to present-day American experience.

Some aspects of early New England life were outrageously intrusive by today's standards. The thoroughgoing cast of Puritan morality seemed to justify an almost totalitarian attitude toward what we would regard as private affairs. Thus, for example, some localities demanded strict accounting of the new settler as to "where he came from, why he came to this country, and whether he brought any estate with him."[2] Throughout the Puritan settlements, tithingmen, the local law-enforcement officers, were expected to concern themselves not only with crimes against persons and property, but also with lapses from strict Puritan morality. Thus they were charged to report

> single persons that live from under Family Government, stubborn and disorderly children and Servants, night-

[1] David H. Flaherty, *Privacy in Colonial New England* (Charlottesville: University Press of Virginia, 1972).
[2] Ibid., p. 172.

> walkers, Typlers, Sabbath breakers, by night or by day, and such as absent themselves from the publick Worship of God on the Lords dayes, or whatever else course or practice of any person or persons whatsoever tending to debauchery, Irreligion, prophaneness, and Atheism amongst us, whether by omission of Family Government, nurture, and religious dutyes, and instruction of Children and Servants, or idle, profligate, uncivil and rude practices of any sort.[3]

Today one would have to go to a commune or a prison to encounter such rigorous surveillance. Yet Flaherty makes it clear that other forces militated against rigorous Puritan principles in these respects. For one thing, Puritan theology itself was ambivalent concerning invasion of privacy. It both justified demands on privacy in some respects and stressed the importance of solitary reflection and self-determination in matters of conscience. But perhaps more important, people often apparently rejected the sharp demands upon privacy dictated by Puritan principle. Such skepticism evidently grew with the passing of time. The enthusiasm of religious feeling declined sharply after the first years in the New World. Informing on one's neighbors had apparently never been a popular duty, and as the militancy of Puritan belief subsided, what we would now regard as "normal" instincts of discretion increasingly asserted themselves.[4] Flaherty provides much anecdotal evidence that meddling in others' affairs became as repugnant to the average eighteenth-century New Englander as it would be to most people today.

An even more profound constraint on invasion of privacy among the early New Englanders stemmed from the structure of colonial society. In their small settlements, the early colonists were physically dispersed. It was common for families to live outside the sight and sound of their nearest neighbors. Although the scarcity of housing and the cold winters forced household units into closer physical intimacy than they would prefer, physical distance insulated such units from intrusive attention from the outside. And Flaherty shows how people

[3] Quoted in ibid., p. 196.
[4] See ibid., p. 17.

sought to improve amenities of privacy within the household, once material conditions permitted.[5]

Moreover, broad categories of demands for personal information simply did not exist in colonial America. Interests beyond the community lacked the resources, both material and organizational, to seek or use data on individuals. Certainly the intrusive claims of one's associates in church, community, or the marketplace could often be distasteful. But the scope of these demands did not stretch further than the network of face-to-face contacts. There were no written forms to fill out for submission to distant offices, no official investigations or dossiers to be completed.

Another work dealing with the origins of present-day privacy controversies is David J. Seipp's *The Right to Privacy in American History*.[6] Like Flaherty's book, Seipp's study counterposes what were apparently rather similar feelings about privacy among Americans in earlier periods with differences in practice stemming from technology and social organization. For example, Seipp notes strong antagonisms early on to such things as eavesdropping and malicious gossip.[7] Like Flaherty, he emphasizes the limitations imposed by physical dispersion and the range of circulation of the spoken word upon the invasion of privacy in early America. He quotes a 19th Century writer as follows:

> As long as gossip was oral, it spread, as regarded any one individual, over a very small area, and was confined to the immediate circle of his acquaintances. It did not reach, or but rarely reached, those who knew nothing of him. It did not make his name, or his walk, or his conversation familiar to strangers.[8]

Like Flaherty, Seipp discusses the mail services as a focus of early privacy-related controversies. The earliest postal services lacked both permanent formal organization and full-time staffs. Both writers describe how, under these circumstances, curious persons managed to keep track of who was writing to

[5] See ibid., Chapter 1.

[6] David J. Seipp, *The Right to Privacy in American History*, Harvard University Program on Information Resources Policy, Publication P-78-3, July 1978.

[7] Ibid., pp. 2–10.

[8] E. L. Godkin, "The Rights of the Citizen.—iv—To His Own Reputation," Scribners, Vol. 8, July 1890; quoted in Seipp., p. 6.

whom, and often of the content of communications as well.[9] Both writers report that the confidentiality of the mails suffered especially during times of war and the threat of it. Clearly the association between extreme demands on personal privacy and overriding "reasons of state" was as strong then as now.

For a long period the mails were the principal means, other than the spoken word, by which personal information might be transmitted. Conflicts intensified in turn, Seipp reports, when the telegraph began to render such information perhaps even more vulnerable than it was in the early mails. Seipp recounts the successful effort of the Lincoln administration to monitor telegraph communications during the early months of the Civil War.[10] He also cites the efforts of the Western Union Company to combat these and other government demands. These struggles to keep the company out of the government surveillance business, however, met with considerable opposition from the Congress. "In the House of Representatives," Seipp reports, "Benjamin F. Butler authorized 'wholesale seizure of telegrams' in his search for evidence to support the impeachment of Andrew Johnson."[11] There seems little doubt that the Western Union's protests against these demands were earnest; Seipp quotes the president of the company's complaint that "agents of this company have been commanded to lay aside the business in which they are engaged to become spies and detectives upon and informers against the customers who have reposed in us the gravest confidence."[12] The controversy ran on for years, with Western Union proposing legislation which would protect telegraphic messages as fully as the mails were by then protected. Instead, Seipp reports, Congress arrived at a compromise which left some such messages open to subpoena, while proscribing wholesale collections of communications of the sort carried out by Lincoln.[13]

[9] See Flaherty, *Privacy in Colonial New England*, pp. 116–17; Seipp, *Right to Privacy*, pp. 10–11.
[10] See Seipp, *Right to Privacy*, pp. 30–31.
[11] Ibid., p 31.
[12] William Orton, in *Congressional Record*, House, 44th Congress, 2nd session, January 5, 1877, p. 353; quoted in Seipp, *Right to Privacy*, p. 32.
[13] Ibid., p. 41.

This shift in focus, from that on the pressures by fellow community members to that on state seizure of telegraph communications, turns on a distinction important to this study. This distinction is much like what the noted sociologist Edward Shils has in mind when he distinguishes between invasion of privacy "by equals within a narrow radius" and that by "those who stand at the center of society, in positions of authority in political, administrative, and cultural institutions."[14]

To be exact, we should note that invasions of privacy such as those noted by Flaherty in early New England need not necessarily be among equals, though they certainly took place among *intimates*. Those who demanded conformity with rigid Puritan morality may have held high standing in the local community. But the implications of these demands were certainly different from those, let us say, of a far-off bureaucracy.

By contrast, the demands of those "who stand at the center of society" are precisely what emerge as we move from the seventeenth and eighteenth to the nineteenth century in America. It is difficult to imagine how such demands could have manifested themselves very strongly during the colonial period. Indeed, the "center" of that society is not easy to identify, and what few central institutions there were hardly were in a position systematically to gather data on the population. But by the Civil War period, all of that had begun to change. For one thing, technologies had developed—telegraphy, in the instance discussed above—which joined different elements to society and which, in the process, made information available to those controlling the technologies. What was noted weakly in the case of the mails, and more sharply of controversies over telegraphy, is something much more central to present-day privacy controversies—the growing availability of personal information from throughout society to those at the center, and the growth of centralized resources to pursue that information. Equally characteristic in Seipp's account of today's privacy controversies, perhaps, is the failure of policy-makers in the mid-nineteenth century

[14] Edward Shils, "Privacy and Power," in *Center and Periphery: Essays in Macrosociology* (Chicago: University of Chicago Press, 1975), pp. 324–25.

to take a decisive stand on who had the rights to obtain and use filed information. The origins of the current privacy issue lie in growing informational intimacy between centralized organizations—including, but not limited to, those of the state—and the balance of the population.

Yet if the forces accounting for such pressures on personal information have changed and grown, the studies by Seipp and Flaherty demonstrate that the sensitivity to the underlying issue was identifiable early on. Alan Westin has established this point well in *Privacy and Freedom.* He writes,

> When the American Republic was founded, the framers established a libertarian equilibrium among the competing values of privacy, disclosure and surveillance. This balance was based on the technological realities of eighteenth-century life. Since torture and inquisition were the only known ways of penetrating the mind, all such measures by government were forbidden by law. Physical entry and eavesdropping were the only means of penetrating private homes and meeting rooms; the framers therefore made eavesdropping by private persons a crime and allowed government to enter private premises only for reasonable searches, under strict warrant controls.[15]

The notion of "equilibrium" here can be misleading, as we argue below. But Westin is right to remind us of the depth of public sensibilities to conflicts over personal data, then and now.

As the nineteenth century wore on, social and technological change generated more and more points of conflict over the use of personal data. One of these, discussed by Westin, Seipp, and a number of other writers, was the rise of the popular press and the perfection of the photographic reproduction processes used by the newspapers. Who had the right to reproduce the image of another, either as news or advertising? When were the affairs of private persons to be considered "out of bounds" for mass publicization? The famous early article on the legal status of privacy by Samuel Warren

[15] Alan F. Westin, *Privacy and Freedom* (New York: Atheneum, 1967), p. 67.

and Louis Brandeis, as is well known, stemmed from their dismay at press reports of social events in the homes of Boston's upper-class families. As they wrote,

> Instantaneous photographs and newspaper enterprise have invaded the sacred precincts of private and domestic life; and numerous mechanical devices threaten to make good the prediction that "what is whispered in the closet shall be proclaimed from the housetops." For years there has been a feeling that the law must afford some remedy for the unauthorized circulation of portraits of private persons; and the evil of the invasion of privacy by the newspapers. . . .[16]

Though they were voices crying in the wilderness at the time, Warren and Brandeis's position subsequently became a major influence on legal thought and practice.

Another point of controversy was the Census. Seipp shows in detail how the Census grew from a relatively simple operation aimed mainly at providing population data for Congressional apportionment to a multipurpose instrument touching on many areas of life. Whereas there was only a single schedule of inquiry containing four questions in the first Census, conducted in 1790, those numbers had risen to six schedules and 142 questions by 1860 and 233 schedules containing a total of 13,161 questions by 1890.[17] A major reason for this expansion was the pressure of business interests for data relevant to pricing and marketing. Another influence was federal government itself, which even as early as the late nineteenth century was beginning to concern itself with fine details of domestic life of the country. Seipp quotes a remarkable statement from the federal Commissioner of Labor in 1887:

> The law making power of the state . . . is constantly called upon to exercise greater and greater supervision

[16] Samuel Warren and Louis D. Brandeis, "The Right to Privacy," *Harvard Law Review*, 4, 1890, p. 195.

[17] Carroll D. Wright, *The History and Growth of the United States Census* (Washington: Government Printing Office, 1900; reprinted New York: Johnson Reprint Corporation, 1966), pp. 85–87. The term "schedule" normally refers to a given set of questions administered to a single class of respondents.

> over the affairs of the people. To do this it has to assume autocratic power. Boards of Health can order private dwellings to be vacated, and the convenience of the individual in such cases is sacrificed to the welfare of the community. This spirit prevails in all directions. The law making branch of our government cannot resist the demands; call it socialism, if you choose, the tendency is as strong as it is perceptible, and as inevitable as it is strong.[18]

It would be difficult to imagine a clearer statement of the intensification of relations between what Shils terms "center" and "periphery" in American life. The implications for privacy are obvious.

[18] Quoted in Seipp, *Right to Privacy*, pp. 29–30.

2 □ Dimensions of Privacy

Thus the emergence of a fundamental, and scarcely surprising, pattern: the development of new ways of recording, transmitting, and using personal information gives rise to new conflicts over such use. All of these conflicts may, in some sense, involve personal privacy, but it must be said that they make up a sociologically rather heterogeneous list. The aversion to seeing one's social life displayed in the popular press stems from concerns different from those underlying the efforts of Western Union and its customers to preserve the confidentiality of telegrams. Moreover, the success or failure of efforts to "protect privacy" in these and other contexts may have much different implications for social relations.

The tendency to treat privacy as if it were a coherent "thing" with the same significance in one setting as in another has often blurred important distinctions. Westin, for example, opened his first book on the subject by drawing parallels between privacy issues in human societies and patterns of animal behavior. He writes,

> . . . virtually all animals seek periods of individual seclusion or small-group intimacy. . . . A meadow pipit chases fellow pipits away from a private space of six feet around him. Except during nesting time, there is only one robin on a bush or branch. The three spined

> stickleback guards an invisible water wall around him and attacks any other stickleback that swims into his territory. . . . Studies of territoriality have even shattered the romantic notion that when robins sing or monkeys shriek, it is solely for the "animal joy of life." Actually, it is often a defiant cry for privacy. . . .[1]

Perhaps it is asking too much of any term to expect it to cover such diverse phenomena as animal territoriality and, let us say, a modern consumer's concern over treatment of his credit records. A fundamental distinction is that between what one might think of as "aesthetic" *versus* "strategic" considerations of privacy.

By *aesthetic* privacy, we mean the restriction of personal information as an end in itself. These are cases where disclosure is inherently embarrassing or distressing. The "instinctive" wish to shield from others acts of excretion, sexual intercourse, or profound emotion involves this form of privacy. If there is any parallel between information-restricting pursuits among humans and those of other animals, it undoubtedly has to do with what we term aesthetic privacy.

What we call *strategic* privacy is the restriction of personal information as a means to some other end. These are instances where privacy facilitates pursuit of other interests. Such cases range from a general's concern to conceal troop movements from the enemy to a father's interest in concealing ambiguous news about his health from his family until matters can be clarified. It includes the wish to conceal future employment plans from one's current employer while seeking a new position elsewhere, or the desire to avoid disclosing to a car salesman the lowest price one is prepared to accept for one's old car in trade. The issue is not the *experience* of disclosing personal information, but the longer-term consequences of doing so.

Among our prehuman ancestors, these two forms of privacy may once have been linked. In other words, creatures may have experienced selective advantage by concealing activities such as excretion, perhaps because such activities acted as a signal to their enemies of their presence. In mod-

[1] Alan F. Westin, *Privacy and Freedom* (New York: Atheneum, 1967), pp. 8–9.

ern human societies, however, the two sensibilities often have very different implications for action, and hence for social relations. Where aesthetic privacy is concerned, we may be willing that others know that the activity takes place, but unwilling that they see or hear it directly. Thus we conceal excretion, but would find it preposterous to deny that it occurs. But strategic privacy is not so much an objection to others' perceiving things at first hand so much as a concern that certain others not draw certain advantages from the information. Thus one may feel no discomfort in telling one's friends of an impending job change, yet wait until a propitious moment to disclose these plans to one's employer and co-workers.

Most conflicts making up the privacy issue in the late twentieth century have to do with strategic considerations. They arise, to simplify only a little, because of new ways in which information about us may affect our interests. Often the information concerned may be banal in itself, hardly the kind of thing which would raise aesthetic-privacy issues. But its possession by specific others, given prevailing social conditions, may pose grave strategic problems.

Similarly, the concerns which make up the privacy issue as it confronts us in the 1970s have mainly to do with what Shils identifies as invasion of privacy by those at the centers of power. That is, they result from the demands for personal information by powerful but more or less distant social entities, ordinarily agencies specializing in information-handling. To be sure, modern technology may provide new ways for private persons motivated simply by malice or perverse curiosity to snoop into the affairs of others, but such instances are relatively rare. The most numerous of modern demands on personal privacy—and the ones which have generated the major current controversies over the matter—have been the demands of powerful government and private organizations.

If we had to offer a single global definition for privacy, we might call it the restriction of others' access to information about oneself. This designation would encompass restrictions for both what we have termed aesthetic and strategic reasons. It points to a distinction of special interest for this book—between social situations in which an individual can choose to disclose rather little about himself and those in which he has little choice but to disclose a great deal. Still, such a sweeping definition leaves open distinctions which must be made before any serious analysis can begin. It lumps indiscriminately, for example, privacy considerations associated with demands of intimates or equals, and those arising from demands of centralized, modern institutions. Both these forms of privacy are important in the context in which they occur, but their sociological properties are quite dissimilar. The concerns of this book have to do with use of personal information—usually in the form of files or computer records—by centralized, authoritative organizations.

3 □ Social Ingredients of the Issue

What is it about modern societies which encourages demands for personal information? While it would be misleading to seek anything so simple as the "cause" for today's privacy controversies, we can specify some necessary, if not sufficient, social conditions for the issue as we confront it today.

One of these conditions, obviously, is the ability to treat information as an independent resource. In nonliterate societies, after all, no form of information can be retained except in someone's memory. One result is that the "informational capital" of such societies, e.g., in the form of folk tradition, is notoriously subject to decay and distortion over time. Obviously the ability to record information and transmit it unaltered represents an enormous adaptive advantage. Even a symbolic system sufficient to record seasons of the year or phases of the moon provides a major gain.

The growth of modern social organization has entailed increasing specialization in the social role of information. In contrast to the simplest societies, modern societies can store very detailed and complex forms of information—far more than could ever be retained within anyone's memory. Perhaps even more important, modern societies develop ways of moving information independent of the movement of persons or goods. In the electronic era, such movement takes place at the speed of light; today we take for granted that computers can exchange enormous amounts of information with each other at such speeds and at minimal costs. Yet these are accomplishments of only the last few decades. To the extent that personal information has taken on "a life of its own"—as a commodity which can be stored, manipulated, transmitted, reinterpreted, and acted on independently of the circumstances in which it first came into existence—all sorts of new conflicts have become possible.

Another sociological concomitant of modern privacy controversies is that most fundamental of all processes of modernization, the specialization of social functions. Students of social change have long considered it axiomatic that modern institutions are, above all, more specialized institutions.[1] Thus as larger societies replace smaller ones, institutions specializing in education come to replace the home or the workplace as mechanisms for transmitting knowledge and skills. Legal systems and other specialized social mechanisms come to replace the effects of community censure and popular justice as means of social control.

The effects of institutional specialization—the growing "division of social labor," in Durkheim's terms—are of course classical themes in the literatures of sociology and anthropology. A key implication of these changes, it is always pointed out, is the growing interdependence of social parts. If the administration of justice becomes delegated to agents of the state, the local community is to this extent less self-sufficient. Likewise, development of factory production and market-oriented agriculture may entail increased efficiency. But these changes place every local community in new relations of dependence with those who constitute other elements of the complicated and complementary social relations involved. Thus modern social systems, more specialized in their institutional arrangements, are to this extent more "systemic." Changes in any one element are much more likely to affect others, and the affairs of the local community respond inevitably, whether the locals prefer it or not, to events elsewhere in the system.

[1] For discussion of the basic principle see Robert L. Carnerio, ed., *The Evolution of Society: Selections from Herbert Spencer's Principles of Sociology* (Chicago: University of Chicago Press, 1967), Introduction; and Lewis A. Coser, *Masters of Sociological Thought* (New York: Harcourt Brace Jovanovich, 1977), pp. 91–93.

The implications of institutional specialization for privacy as defined above are varied. On the one hand, the growth of larger-scale, more internally specialized social systems certainly frees individuals from all sorts of localized pressures on personal information. Specialized institutions ordinarily deal with limited portions of people's social lives—e.g., someone is a worker at the factory, a member of the congregation at church, a member at the lodge, a husband and father at home. In modern, internally specialized social systems, such roles and their demands may be more or less segregated from one another. This fact, coupled with the sheer size and relative anonymity of larger, more modern social systems, yields *gains* for privacy as the scale of social life grows. The loosening of privacy-eroding demands from neighbors and kinfolk has often been noted in this connection. On the other hand, the specialized institutions of modern societies have their own demands to make for personal information, both from those who work in them and from the publics which they serve. These demands hold special interest here.

Perhaps the most characteristically modern of all differentiated, specialized social institutions is the formal organization. Formal organizations are social entities designed to accomplish specific things according to accountable rules. The "rational" or efficiency-maximizing style of action characteristic of such institutions now predominates in government, business, voluntary associations, the professions, and countless other spheres of organized action. The life of modern societies is so thoroughly dependent on formally constituted organizations that hardly any human activity, from courtship and reproduction to warfare, can take place without them.

To be sure, formal organizations are not the only social structures which perform complex and essential tasks. Such things as kinship systems are indispensable in organizing the activities of many societies, yet no one deliberately *organizes* kinship relations—they merely "grow up." Likewise, markets of various kinds organize the activities of very large numbers of people, often in a highly "rational" way; yet markets differ fundamentally from formal organizations. In a market, people's bidding for prices may have the effect of moving large amounts of goods or services and setting what are in some sense optimal prices for them. But no one "plans" the prices or compels the actors to play their parts. For many people, this is the overriding charm of market systems.

By contrast, in bureaucratic systems, people's actions are coordinated not so much by their doing what "comes naturally" as by their fulfilling the requirements of roles which exist independent of their incumbency. In principle, bureaucracies are like machines, whose overall output is made predictable through the predictable interrelations of each part within them. Of course, every sociologist appreciates how far particular bureaucracies deviate from this principle. But the fact remains that no other form of social structure embodies such thoroughgoing principles of goal-oriented efficiency.

Formal organizations bind their members into systems of determinate action. In other words, every organization embodies relationships wherein orders given at one point are binding on the actions of others. Here again, as everyone knows, bureaucracies often fall far short of the mark, and messages from the top go astray, are subverted, or are simply ignored elsewhere in the system. But bureaucracies do develop decision-making centers which may set in motion far-reaching chains of action. Societies in which formal organizations are well developed thus seem as though "strung together" by organizational action systems.

4 □ An "Organized" World

Thus even in the most remote communities in present-day America one would find people with commitments to distant formal organizations. The postmaster, local police officials, insurance agents, local clergymen in their affiliation with parent churches—all such persons bear such commitments. In these ties we see concrete manifestations of the interdependence of social parts in modern societies. These ties should remind us how thoroughly America, like other advanced societies, has become "organized" by comparison to its social structure of past centuries.

By contrast, the involvement by Americans in formal organizations of any kind early in the last century was miniscule. In 1816, the total civilian employment of the federal government—undoubtedly the largest formal organization of the time in America—was 4,500. About one-third of these were postal officials. By 1851, total employment by the federal government had risen to 25,713, with some 21,391 in the postal service. By contrast, civilian employment of the federal government came to nearly 3 million persons in 1970. This amounts to some 1.5 percent of the total population as against about 0.05 percent in 1816.

Thus, although Americans clearly shared a strong national consciousness from early on in their history, the present ascendance of formal organization is a relatively recent thing.

Allan Nevins, writing of America just before the Civil War, has noted,

> The farmers were unorganized. Labor was unorganized. Professional groups, apart from the clergy and physicians, were unorganized. Retail business was unorganized. To observant men, the country seemed invertebrate. National authority was still poorly centralized in any of its numerous offices. It might be set at naught in almost any area by the imperfections of its machinery, the clashing authority of the States, and the high-tempered individualism of the citizens.[1]

Nevins points to business enterprises as the main exceptions to these trends—"islands of organization," he calls them, "in a restless sea of multitudinous unorganized activities."[2] But by modern standards, the numbers of persons employed by the early corporations were paltry.

By contrast, modern Americans inhabit a social environment virtually composed of formal organizations. The main source of the privacy controversies of the 1960s and 1970s has been the demands of formal organizations for information on the people with whom these organizations must deal. Each major life juncture seems to entail involvement of some formal organization. Birth, immunization, education, military service, marriage and divorce, the use of credit and insurance, home ownership, medical care, and, ultimately, death—these and countless other key life events require the participation of formal organizations. And such participation almost always seems to require collection of information on the persons concerned. Sometimes the information serves to mark a key event of life—a birth, immunization or treatment for a disease, educational attainments, etc. Elsewhere information helps organizations to distinguish what treatment is to be accorded the individual. The development of these personal documentation practices, and that of the organizations maintaining them, is in many cases quite recent.

One of the most basic and long-standing forms of personal documentation is the *registration and certification of vital events*. The early colonists brought with them from England

[1] Allan Nevins, *Ordeal of the Union*, Vol. II (New York: Scribner, 1947), p. 245.
[2] Ibid., p. 246.

the custom of parish registry of births, deaths, and marriages. But uniform recording of these events by the state for most of the population has come about only in the early decades of this century. One of the earliest state registration laws dates from 1795 in Massachusetts.[3] It required parents to report to the town clerk births and deaths of children, and householders to report such events in their households. Such early legislation, both in Massachusetts and elsewhere, must have been very unevenly effective. Probably the great majority of all vital events in rural areas of the country remained unregistered until at least the late nineteenth century.

In 1903, Congress passed a joint resolution requesting state authorities to cooperate with the Census Bureau to develop a uniform system of registration nationwide. Federal authorities organized this work by seeking to develop "registration areas" for births and deaths. These were to be areas where at least 90 percent of such events were recorded. As the tables here show, it was not until 1933 that this basic level of coverage extended to the entire country.

Today, by contrast, nearly all states maintain close to total coverage, not only of births and deaths, but also of marriages and divorces. Nearly every birth is registered and nearly everyone has a birth certificate.[4] The exigencies of modern social life make possession of such documents essential, so much so that we forget how recent the nearly universal reliance on such certification really is. And federal authorities, whether they realized it or not, acted to create a world suited to their own needs when they promoted the extension of registration. It is believed that the federal government itself accounts directly or indirectly for about half of today's demands for these certifications.[5]

Passports are obviously another key personal document for many people today. As with birth and death certification, the principle of passport issuance goes well back in history, but their use on a mass scale is a modern phenomenon.

[3] This discussion is based upon U.S. Dept. of Health, Education and Welfare, *Vital Statistics of the United States*, Vol. I (Washington D.C.: U.S. Government Printing Office, 1950), pp. 2–19.

[4] In our own survey of the general public in Long Island, New York, some 90 percent of 291 respondents reported having birth certificates in their possession.

[5] This estimate was provided by an official of the Department of Health, Education and Welfare Vital Statistics Division.

TABLE 1
YEAR OF STATES' ADMISSION TO THE BIRTH REGISTRATION AREA

Year	State
1915	Connecticut
	Maine
	Massachusetts
	Michigan
	Minnesota
	New Hampshire
	New York
	Pennsylvania
	Rhode Island[1]
	Vermont
	District of Columbia[2]
1916	Maryland
1917	Indiana
	Kansas
	Kentucky
	North Carolina
	Ohio
	Utah
	Virginia
	Washington
	Wisconsin
1919	California
	Oregon
	South Carolina[3]
1920	Nebraska
1921	Delaware
	Mississippi
	New Jersey
1922	Illinois
	Montana
	Wyoming
1924	Florida
	Iowa
	North Dakota
1925	West Virginia
1926	Arizona
	Idaho
1927	Alabama
	Arkansas
	Louisiana
	Missouri
	Tennessee
1928	Colorado
	Georgia
	Oklahoma
1929	Nevada
	New Mexico
1932	South Dakota
1933	Texas

[1] Dropped from the birth-registration area in 1919; readmitted in 1921.
[2] Included in states.
[3] Dropped from the birth-registration area in 1925; readmitted in 1928.
SOURCE: *Vital Statistics of the United States*, p. 14.

TABLE 2
YEAR OF STATES' ADMISSION TO THE DEATH REGISTRATION AREA

Year	State	Year	State
1880	Massachusetts	1911	Kentucky
	New Jersey		Missouri
	District of Columbia[1]	1913	Virginia
		1914	Kansas
1890	Connecticut	1916	South Carolina
	Delaware[2]	1917	Tennessee
	New Hampshire	1918	Illinois
	New York		Louisiana
	Rhode Island		Oregon
	Vermont	1919	Florida
1900	Maine		Mississippi
	Michigan	1920	Nebraska
	Indiana	1922	Georgia[5]
1906	California		Idaho
	Colorado		Wyoming
	Maryland	1923	Iowa
	Pennsylvania	1924	North Dakota
	South Dakota[3]	1925	Alabama
1908	Washington		West Virginia
	Wisconsin	1926	Arizona
1909	Ohio	1927	Arkansas
1910	Minnesota	1928	Oklahoma
	Montana	1929	Nevada
	North Carolina[4]		New Mexico
	Utah	1933	Texas

[1] Included in states.
[2] Dropped from the registration area in 1900; readmitted in 1919.
[3] Dropped from the registration area in 1910; readmitted in 1930.
[4] Included only municipalities with populations of 1,000 or more in 1900 (about 16 percent of the total population); the remainder of the state was added to the area in 1916.
[5] Dropped from the registration area in 1925; readmitted in 1928.
SOURCE: *Vital Statistics of the United States*, p. 14.

Passports have been issued in America since colonial times; for a time both states and the federal government issued passports.[6] But their use was not required until World War I, and until then many travelers apparently did not bother to obtain them at all. The requirement to use a passport was relaxed once again between the world wars, and then for a time after World War II. Only since 1952, when the Immigration and Nationality Act came into law, have passports been required in peacetime.

During the eight years James Madison served as Secretary of State, from 1801 to 1809, the State Department issued only about 600 passports. By contrast, the total figure of new passports issued and renewed in 1911 was 22,757, and the equivalent figure for 1977 is more than 3 million. The total number of valid passports in effect in 1977 was in excess of 13 million.

Matching this growth in coverage of the population has been the intensification of informational demands. Prior to 1850, the State Department required only proof of citizenship for passport issuance. Such proof could consist of a letter from the applicant, certification from a notary public, or a letter from a third person known to the Department of State. The application for 1889 required name, date and place of birth, address, occupation, date of departure, country to be visited, purpose of the trip, and a physical description. In 1905, the State Department introduced further requirements for obtaining a passport, including a birth certificate or other proof of citizenship. In 1914 a photograph was required for the first time. 1955 saw the addition of further demands for information from applicants, including questions on Communist party affiliation, though a Supreme Court decision ended the latter requirement in 1959. At the time of this writing, the passport application requires answers to over forty questions, including queries on such things as parents' birthplace and previous marriages. Recent privacy legislation, inciden-

[6] Information in this section is derived from personal communication with the Passport Office of the State Department; from U.S. Dept of State, *The United States Passport: Past, Present, Future* (Washington, D.C.: U.S. Government Printing Office, 1976); and from U.S. Dept. of State, "Summary of Passport Statistics (Passport Office, Bureau of Consumer Affairs, 1978).

tally, has resulted in the classification of a few of these questions as "not mandatory."

Since 1967, some passport records have been computerized; since 1978 all new application files have been stored on microfilm. Passport officials work closely in exchanging personal data with agents of many other arms of the federal government, including the Internal Revenue Service, the FBI, and the CIA.

Another key form of personal documentation for most Americans is the *driver's license.* States have required the purchase of licenses since as early as 1903, but at first only as a revenue-generating measure.[7] In many cases one simply purchased the license over the counter in a store, much as one would a fishing license. Use of driving licenses as a measure to regulate driving behavior began only as the numbers of vehicles began to mount. As with other major personal-record systems, both the coverage and the intensity of information exchange in driver licensing have grown rapidly since early this century. Today there are approximately 137 million licensed drivers throughout the country. The first licensing practices required little personal data from the applicant. Today, the licenses of virtually all states display the driver's name, address, date of birth, and signature. In addition, the licenses of forty-seven states show the bearer's height, forty-one show weight, thirty-eight show eye color, and thirty show the Social Security number. Eleven use the Social Security number as the driving-license serial number. Information stored in state files considerably exceeds what is shown on the license itself. Each year insurance companies spend millions of dollars to cull personal information from these state files, including data on accidents, traffic offenses, license suspensions and revocations, and other personal information on the driver.

The record systems associated with driver licensing afford extensive and sophisticated data exchange among interested agencies. In 1960, for example, Congress established the National Driver Register for exchange of data among states. The

[7] Sources for this discussion are personal communications with the American Association of Motor Vehicle Administrators and U.S. Department of Justice, *The Report of the Federal Advisory Committee on False Identification* (Washington, D.C.: U.S. Government Printing Office, 1976).

register serves mainly to curtail reregistration in other states by those convicted of driving violations. Facilitating these and other forms of information exchange has been the steady computerization of driving-license records. Sixty percent of all driver records throughout the country are now available on a computer-to-computer basis, both to other driving-license agencies and to law-enforcement organizations. In 1976, the National Law Enforcement Telecommunications System exchanged some 1.3 million such computerized messages.

As everyone knows, driver's licenses are such fundamental parts of one's public identity these days that their importance extends well beyond the realm of driving. It has become the closest thing we have to an "identity card" in America. So pervasive are demands for presentation of the driving license as a means of identification that all but seventeen states now issue "non-driver's licenses" to those who do not drive, but who need the documentation in order to make their way in a document-oriented world.

Reliance on *consumer credit* in America today is almost as widespread as that on the automobile. Whenever someone seeks to open a credit account or make a purchase on credit, the credit grantor routinely buys a report on the applicant from a credit bureau.[8] The content of that report is intended to provide a balanced and varied profile on the applicant's ability and willingness to meet the obligations in question.

Use of consumer credit and of credit cards is so pervasive in present-day America that it is practically impossible to avoid having a credit record, or to escape the effects of that record. Yet like other record systems noted here, the consumer-credit system was hardly recognizable before the beginning of the present century. People did buy on credit before that time, but local reputation and face-to-face acquaintance apparently sufficed to establish credit worthiness. The first credit bureaus were simple "black lists" of bad debts pooled among department stores, so that credit would not be extended to those who had failed to pay before. From these unre-

[8] The information in this section, unless otherwise noted, is from numerous field interviews conducted by the authors between 1967 and 1978 with officials in the credit industry, and from National Commission on Consumer Finance, *Consumer Credit in the United States* (Washington, D.C.: U.S. Government Printing Office, 1972).

TABLE 3

GROWTH IN CONSUMER CREDIT, 1900–1976

Year	Total Consumer Debt[1] (Estimated in Billions of Dollars)
1900	1.0
1912	2.9
1920	3.0
1930	6.4
1940	8.3
1950	21.5
1960	56.1
1970	126.8
1976	217.8

[1] Installment and non-installment consumer debt, excluding mortgages.
Sources: For 1900–1912: United States Department, Bureau of the Census, *Historical Statistics of the United States* (Washington, D.C.: U.S. Government Printing Office, 1975), p. 253; for 1920–1970, Ibid., p. 1009; for 1976, United States Department of Commerce, Bureau of the Census, *Statistical Abstracts of the United States* (Washington, D.C.: U.S. Government Printing Office, 1977), p. 534. Beginning with 1960, data include Alaska and Hawaii.

markable beginnings, the credit-reporting industry has grown in pace with the growth in consumer credit itself, as shown in Table 3.

Modern credit-bureau files entail much more than simple compilations of bad debts. Depending on the bureau, the files comprise data on the consumer's job and employer, place of residence, marital status and history, income, assets, liabilities, and matters such as bankruptcies, liens, tax judgments, and the like. In addition, modern credit bureaus seek to develop the most comprehensive possible account of the consumer's recent use of credit—the amounts borrowed, the nature of the credit accounts, and the promptness of payment.

An official of the Associated Credit Bureaus, the national trade association, has estimated that 150 million credit histories were on file in America's credit bureaus in 1977. This figure counts many individuals more than once, because of the inclusion of people's files in more than one bureau at a time. On the other hand, many married couples are covered in single credit histories. Since the 1960s credit reporting has been increasingly computerized. The computer system of TRW Credit Data, one of the largest on-line computer systems in the country, in 1977 held information on an estimated 70 million consumers, and was capable of generating more than 200,000 credit reports daily.[9] TRW Credit Data sold over 22 million credit reports in 1977.[10]

Similar to the personal-record system sustaining consumer credit, but even less well understood in the public mind, is that associated with *insurance*. Most insurance firms, like credit grantors, prefer to scrutinize applicants for coverage in advance. There are a number of reasons for this. In life insurance, the insurer wishes to avoid selling to persons whose health or whose way of life would make a claim especially likely. In automobile coverage, most firms seek to avoid doing business with persons regarded as disreputable within their communities. Prejudice on the part of the firm is not necessarily the reason for this. When such persons become involved in litigation over damage or injury claims, the firms believe they are liable to fare poorly before juries, regardless of the merits of the case.

These concerns have given rise to a little-known industry

[9] *Press Handbook on Consumer Credit Reporting* (Long Beach, Calif.: TRW Credit Data, 1977), p. 41. "On line" computing is that where the user is in direct interaction with the computor memory, and thus can receive immediate responses to inquiries made, for example, from a keyboard console.

[10] TRW Credit Data does not release information on credit-report sales volume. We were told that the firm processed 452,994 consumer inquiries in 1977, and elsewhere it is reported, "Less than 2 percent of the reports [issued by TRW Credit Data] result in a consumer inquiry" (ibid., p. 9). It is reasonable to assume that consumer inquiries involved 1 to 2 percent of reports, and that the company thus sold between 22 and 45 million credit reports.

specializing in compiling records relevant to people's insurability. These firms sell their "products"—reports on the persons concerned—to insurance companies; they also sell similar reports on prospective employees to employers. To research the reports, they maintain staffs of field investigators who interrogate neighbors, friends, associates, and co-workers of the applicant. Like credit bureaus, these firms had their beginning around the turn of the century. It is difficult to enumerate the extent of their business exactly. But the largest of the firms, Equifax, employed in 1977 some 13,000 persons, sold approximately 30 million investigative reports, and maintained some 145 million files.[11]

The United States had no national law-enforcement body, and hence no nationally centralized criminal records, until the founding of the FBI in 1908. Today the FBI maintains the fingerprints of some 63 million people.[12] Fewer than half of these have been convicted of a crime. The FBI also keeps detailed personal dossiers on more than six million persons, by no means all of them criminals.

In 1967 the FBI instituted its National Crime Information Center. This is a computerized system of information exchange on crime and criminals, for use by law-enforcement agencies throughout the United States and Canada. It provides direct contact to eighty-six terminals from the central data file, with a data base of some 6 million items of information. Users may interrogate the system for information on such things as stolen property, wanted and missing persons, and the criminal records of individual offenders. The system can usually provide a response to a given inquiry within a few seconds.

Death and taxes may be inevitable, but the sophisticated personal record-keeping associated with modern *income taxation* is a relatively recent social phenomenon. After twice

[11] Although this industry continues to flourish, it is interesting to note that some leading insurance companies seem to be relying on insurance reporting less and less. For reasons which may be a mixture of cost consciousness, privacy concern, and skepticism about the quality of reports, these companies have been developing alternative bases for judgment on insurance applicants.

[12] Information in this discussion was derived from personal communication with FBI officials.

being instituted and discontinued, the personal-income tax was established by Congressional action in 1913.[13] In that year, the Bureau of Internal Revenue, as it was called, had some 4,000 employees and accounted for about $344 million in revenue. The equivalent figures for 1970 were 60,000 employees and $200 billion.

The present very wide coverage of the American population by IRS record-keeping is particularly recent. Until shortly before World War II, relatively few citizens were income-tax payers—about 8 million immediately before the war, as compared to 60 million in wartime. Over 85 million personal-income-tax returns were filed in 1977, many of them joint returns. Among the data maintained in IRS files are taxpayer's and spouse's Social Security numbers, name of spouse, selected financial information from the tax return, past tax assessments, debit and credit transactions between the IRS and the taxpayer, and audit history.[14]

Computerization of IRS records began in 1961, with the opening of the National Computer Center in Martinsburg, West Virginia. Computing now plays a major role in helping to detect tax fraud. In 1970 the IRS began to develop on-line computing, and by 1975, 3,200 data-retrieval terminals were in use in IRS service centers and field offices. These provide virtually instantaneous access to certain tax-return data, though taxpayers' files have not been fully computerized at the time of this writing. On an average day the terminals handle more than a million requests.[15]

Social Security came into existence in 1936. Its inception brought about a surge of IRS activities, since that agency was designated to collect the payroll taxes which supported Social Security programs. During the first year of its existence, Social Security issued numbers to, and instituted records on,

[13] This discussion is based on John C. Chommie, *The Internal Revenue Service* (New York: Praeger, 1970), pp. 16–19.
[14] Internal Revenue Service, *ADP in IRS*, Training publication 2426-01 (Washington, D.C.: U.S. Government Printing Office, 1975), pp. 8, 97–98; Internal Revenue Service, *Annual Report 1977* (Washington, D.C.: U.S. Government Printing Office, 1977), p. 17.
[15] Chommie, *Internal Revenue Service*, pp. 28–29; Internal Revenue Service, "Integrated Data Retrieval System," Publication 785 (Washington, D.C.: U.S. Government Printing Office, 1976), pp. 3–13.

some 45 million people.[16] Today the system maintains records on some 140 million living Americans. Contents of these files obviously vary greatly. But most files maintain data on basic matters such as name, date of birth, sex, race, yearly earnings, work history, and benefit history. Under certain circumstances, Social Security files may also include data on circumstances surrounding eligibility for benefits, alcoholism or drug addiction, financial resources other than earned income, etc.

In 1943, President Roosevelt issued an executive order establishing the Social Security number as an identifier for all federal-agency files. Since that time, countless other public and private organizations have seized upon the Social Security number as an identifier for their files. As a result, the Social Security card has become one of our basic personal documents in America, needed for all sorts of purposes having little to do with Social Security. The Social Security file, as distinct from the card, has by the same token become a source of personal data for other government agencies.

Not all of the centralized forms of personal record-keeping mentioned above were wholly unprecedented at their inception; some undoubtedly duplicated and perhaps supplanted more localized forms of accounting. We have already noted that some localized forms of birth, death, and marriage certification existed even before the nineteenth century. Likewise, significant repositories of law-enforcement information may have existed in local or state jurisdictions before the FBI began its nationwide accounting. However, because of their dispersion, the extent of these earlier forms of accounting is inherently difficult to assess. In cases like registration of vital events, the institutions carrying out the record-keeping existed but were incapable of reaching all those now covered. In cases like income taxation, Social Security, and insurance reporting, the organizations which now carry out the record-keeping simply had not yet been founded.

Nor do all the different institutions mentioned above

[16] Alan F. Westin and Michael A. Baker, *Databanks in a Free Society* (New York: Quadrangle/The New York Times Book Company, 1972), p. 33.

play the same roles in creating and using personal documentation. The registration of vital events, for example, produces documented personal information for use in a wide variety of other settings, but does not dispense benefits to the public other than the documentation itself. By contrast, credit grantors provide services desired by the public through scrutiny of documentary information generated elsewhere; one might consider credit grantors mainly "consumers" of personal documentation. A third kind of institution is the insurance-reporting or credit-reporting firm—a kind of intermediary between institutions which are primarily producers and those which are primarily consumers of documented personal data. Such institutions have become especially controversial since the 1960s. Their role as specialists in collecting and transmitting personal data relevant to decision-making on the people concerned multiplies their importance in people's lives and, commensurately, the potential for conflict over their activities.

What makes any classification in these matters tenuous, however, is that organizations play different roles in different phases of their work. Credit-granting firms, for example, act as "consumers" of documentary information when they seek data in evaluating credit applications. But they are also "producers" of personal documentation for other credit grantors, who use the data to make yet further decisions on the same applicants. Similarly, the Passport Office of the State Department is a consumer of documentation in screening passport applications. But in providing the passport, it acts as a producer of documentation to other agencies. Perhaps the one clear point in all this is that the requirements of formal organizations for personal documentation feed on one another. Organizations demand authoritative information on the people with whom they deal, and these demands give rise to other formal organizations to provide this information. These new organizations typically must authenticate the personal data which they use for their own decision-making purposes, and so a new cycle of demands begins.

Simply to characterize this new reality as reflecting the appetite of organizations for personal information would be accurate, but would miss much of the significance of these changes.[17] The growth of these systems reflects *new relationships* between ordinary Americans and formal organizations. These new relationships entail sociologically distinctive sets of demands and pressures among the parties. People expect organizations to deal "appropriately" with literally millions of persons. In every case, the organization is expected to render to each individual his or her precise "due"—that is, the correct form of bureaucratic action, in light of that person's past history and current situation. Clearly such discriminating decision-making can only take place through reliance on detailed personal information.

Income taxation, for example, entails assessment of the precise liability of each taxpayer, liability reckoned in terms of amount of income, dependency status, assets and losses during the tax year, and a host of other circumstances. Given that payment of taxes is a distasteful obligation and that most persons strive to avoid paying any more than necessary, any system of enforcement will face pressures to collect and use voluminous data. Such data not only enable the IRS to assess the obligation to pay, but also provide the basis on which to adjudicate disputes with taxpayers and to locate those judged delinquent or suspect. The same observations could be offered for most other bureaucratic personal-data systems which have sprung up since the last century. Consumer-credit data files, for example, enable credit-granting organizations to assess precisely how much credit should be extended. Insurance-reporting systems afford insurance companies sophisticated bases for discriminating judgments about whether to insure people, and if so, at what rates. Law-enforcement records enable these organizations to distinguish in their treatment of the literally millions of persons with whom they deal every year, according to the kinds of action which they "deserve."

This characterization does not apply to absolutely all uses of personal documentation by modern organizations. The enormous numbers of personal checks processed by banks, for example, involve decision-making only in the abstract sense of the decision to debit an account when the check is

[17] For discussion of a number of these issues, see Edward Shils' remarks on the "cognitive passion" of government and related demands on privacy in "Privacy and Power" in his book of collected essays, *Center and Periphery: Essays in Macrosociology* (Chicago: University of Chicago Press, 1975).

processed. But most personal records created and used by modern bureaucracies serve to guide subsequent bureaucratic decisions over how to treat the people depicted in the files.

The most dramatic cases of the role of personal documentation in shaping organizational treatment of people involve very large, obviously powerful organizations. The impact in the public mind of the literally millions of FBI dossiers, for example, with their uncertain but worrisome effect on people's employment opportunities, has been a major ingredient of the privacy issue. But smaller organizations also rely on personal information. A small bank or loan company relies on credit reports and other documentation in processing loan requests just as much as do its giant counterparts. A small employer may rely as heavily as a giant corporation on the report of an insurance- and employment-reporting firm, or for that matter on the records of a law-enforcement agency, in screening job applicants. Both large and small organizations have the power to extend or deny jobs or credit, to assess and enforce tax obligations, or to sell or decline insurance business. And both large and small organizations rely on personal-record systems for these purposes.

Sociologists have often characterized formal organizations as systems for coping with *uncertainty* in their environments.[18] All organizations must keep track of more or less unpredictable aspects of their environments—making plans, adjustments, and rearrangements and the like so as to achieve their desired results. If the aim is, for example, to sell automobiles at a profit, then the organization must attend to variations in supplies of raw materials, costs of power, fluctuations in demand, availability of labor, and many other things in order to do so. If the aim is the administration of a church diocese, central management must monitor the attitudes of the clergy, the faithfulness of the communicants, the costs of maintaining the physical plant, the attitudes of the larger community toward the church, and many other potential sources of uncertainty. Again, formal organizations are not the only social forms which coordinate and facilitate human action in the face of otherwise uncertain conditions. But

[18] See Charles Perrow, *Complex Organizations: A Cri'ical Essay* (Glenview, Ill.: Scott, Foresman and Co., 1972), p. 173 and James D. Thompson, *Organizations in Action* (New York: McGraw-Hill, 1967).

only formal organizations in the modern sense devote themselves so systematically and self-consciously to searching for unpredictable or disruptive elements in the environment, and attempting to master them so as to achieve desired results.

For the organizational activities of interest here, the environment is people; the uncertainties to be mastered are ambiguities as to what people "deserve" what organizational responses. Modern income-taxation systems, for example, are charged with enforcing an obligation according to complex principles, in the light of circumstances which differ in every case. Not only must such systems apply these principles to such heterogeneous cases; they must also reckon with people's often strenuous efforts to withhold information. To confront this "blooming, buzzing confusion" of people's financial affairs and enforce a modicum of compliances—this entails real mastery of uncertainty. Likewise for other organizations which systematically demand and use personal information in dealing with very large publics. The IRS and other organizations can no more do without authoritative information on the people with whom they deal than can General Motors meet its goals without certain kinds of data—data about the costs of raw materials, the demand for finished automobiles, costs of transportation, and the thousands of uncertain circumstances which make formal organizations necessary in the first place.

5 □ Surveillance and Social Control

Systems of detailed personal records do not *always* appear when organizations deal with large numbers of people. Instead, they develop under conditions of complex obligations and extended mutual dependency between organizations and their publics. In *Private Lives and Public Surveillance*, Rule characterized these conditions as most propitious:

> 1. When an agency must regularly deal with a clientele too large and anonymous to be kept track of on a basis of face-to-face acquaintance;
>
> 2. When these dealings entail the enforcement of rules advantageous to the agency and potentially burdensome to the clientele;
>
> 3. When these enforcement activities involve decision-making about how to act towards the clientele . . .
>
> 4. When the decisions must be made discriminatingly, according to precise details of each person's past history or present situation;
>
> 5. When the agency must associate every client with what it considers the full details of his past history, es-

> pecially so as to forestall people's evading the consequences of their past behavior.[1]

Thus Yankee Stadium will require no detailed documentation on ticket purchasers, despite variation in ticket prices and seat assignment. But where organizations enter into relationships enduring over time, whose outcomes must be geared to details of people's lives, the recourse to personal-data systems is very likely.

We call the systematic monitoring of personal data *surveillance*. We use this term in a neutral sense to indicate monitoring for all sorts of purposes, both helpful and coercive. The purpose of surveillance we call *social control*. Here again, we make no value judgment in the use of the term. We mean by social control any means of influence by which a person or an organization seeks to render other people's behavior or circumstances more predictable and more acceptable. Social control in this sense includes everything from exhortations on the ethical superiority of good behavior to provision of organizational manuals specifying what good behavior entails in particular circumstances. It includes both coercive measures, such as shooting the opposition, and benign processes, such as maintaining preventive health care among one's work force. We must emphasize that "surveillance" and "social control" need not entail what people would regard as manipulation or repression. Application of influence to keep social processes working satisfactorily, and attention to the behavior of those who make up these processes, are universal facts of social life. We may find them essential under some conditions, abhorrent in others; but without some measure of them, organized social life would grind to a halt.

Thus we define social control quite broadly. The forms of social control discussed in this book, however, most often have to do with the enforcement of norms. That is, surveillance systems discussed here work mainly to monitor compliance with standards of behavior, and to enable organizations to promote what they deem desirable social conditions or practices.

The enforcement activities which require surveillance may

[1] James B. Rule, *Private Lives and Public Surveillance* (New York: Schocken, 1974), p. 29. The following section recapitulates some of the theoretical discussions in the earlier book.

take many different forms. One of the most cost-effective is to exclude troublesome people from participation. Thus a key goal in consumer credit is to avoid extending credit at all to those considered poor risks. Taking people "out of circulation" plays an important role in many systems. The forms taken by this strategy range from simply declining applications, in credit and other areas, to throwing people in jail, to executing them.

Another technique of social control is to adjust the privileges accorded to individuals to the risks which they pose for the controllers. Thus when a credit organization does extend credit, it will attempt to tailor the amount and nature of the privileges to its reading of what is "safe" in the case of the person concerned. Such judgments obviously require recourse to detailed personal data in the service of what we term "fine-grained decision-making." Record-keeping organizations, in seeking to control welfare payments, income-tax collections, law-enforcement actions, personnel matters, and countless other applications of organizational resources, find it essential to use personal data in making decisions.

A third method of social control is to reach out actively to curtail behavior considered undesirable. Credit-card systems, when their relations with card holders go bad, end up dispatching an agent to confiscate the card or even to arrest the person. The IRS, of course, can arrest and prosecute in extreme cases. So can welfare systems, if fraud is established, and so, of course, can all sorts of law-enforcement systems. The recourse to actual coercion is rare, however, in systems like those studied here. It is, after all, very costly. When organizations must resort to it, it ordinarily means that more subtle, routine forms of influence have failed.

We have been discussing formal organizations. But both social control and surveillance, in other forms, are standard ingredients of all social life, even in the most intimate settings. We all pay close attention to the actions and characteristics of those around us; we all adjust the trust which we extend and the ways in which we attempt to influence others' actions to what we know about them. And if others' actions strike us as especially threatening to our wishes or interests, we may even resort to coercion, although this is usually as desperate an expedient in face-to-face relations as in the dealings of bureaucracies with their publics.

The highly specialized facilities of modern organizations, with their massive data files and highly routinized practices for dealing with their publics, thus need not seem bizarre. Their seemingly unique activities have their counterparts in everyday life. The sweeping intake of personal information by these organizations and its sophisticated use in fashioning pertinent, forceful responses to the persons concerned represent a response to public expectations of bureaucratic action. Members of the publics served by these organizations expect them to provide just the "correct" response to each person, much as an individual would do in his or her face-to-face dealings with others. People expect, or indeed demand, to have their "records" taken into account in fixing their eligibility for credit, or their entitlement to Social Security, or their income-tax obligations, or their educational opportunities. And this necessitates recourse to personal-data systems. For while memory may serve as an adequate "data base" in dealings with personal acquaintances, only systematic documentary records-keeping can suffice for the needs of organizations.

But the sheer amount of information required is not the only reason for recourse to documentation. Even if some extraordinary bureaucrat could retain all the data used for decision-making on individuals in his or her head, documentation would still be necessary. For the written word—or the retrievable computer file—represents the ideal medium for bureaucratic action. People who work in bureaucracies must be able to show—to their superiors or to inquiring outsiders—that they did the "right" thing under "all the circumstances." And this places a premium on documentation. Hence the well-known reflex in formal organizations to create a written record of every action for which the official could conceivably be held accountable.

It is no exaggeration to describe modern organizations as engaged in the "production" of authoritative decisions about people, or to characterize personal information as the "raw material" for this production. We may think of particular bureaucracies as law-enforcement agencies, or social-insurance organizations, or credit grantors, or personnel systems, or national-security systems, or systems of medical-care delivery. But all of these are involved in discriminating decision-making as to which persons require what applications of organizational resources.[2] The specialization of such decision-making on a very large scale by formal organizations—and the dependency of the great majority of the population upon such decision-making—is one of the distinctive sociological features of highly developed societies.

[2] In a similar vein, another writer has noted the rising importance in modern society "of those organizations whose explicit function is not to change the behavior of people directly but to process them and confer public statuses on them. . . . These organizations shape a person's life by controlling his access to a wide range of social settings through the public status they confer. . . ." Yeheskel Hasenfeld, "People Processing Organizations: An Exchange Approach," *American Sociological Review*, Vol. 37, June 1972.

6 □ The Twentieth Century

The steady development of these documentary systems, however, did not immediately incite public consciousness or concern. Indeed, the present salience of organizational record-keeping as a privacy issue had its origins remarkably recently. The "privacy issues" of the early twentieth century appear in retrospect as discontinuous skirmishes over various uses of personal data.

Throughout the twentieth century, as before, controversies have followed innovations in such uses. As new ways of creating, transmitting, and using data on people—bureaucratically or otherwise—came into currency, conflicts inevitably swirled around the propriety of these uses. One series of such controversies early this century had to do with uses of people's names and likenesses in advertising. Arthur R. Miller describes how New York courts grappled with this question in a 1902 case. A young woman found her picture disseminated in the advertising of a flour, and sued the milling company for the "humiliation" which she thus suffered.[1] Miller notes that the court sympathized with the plaintiff, but nevertheless took the conservative position that her privacy was not protected under common law. In so doing, the court expressly

[1] Arthur R. Miller, *The Assault on Privacy* (Ann Arbor, Mich.: University of Michigan Press, 1971), p. 171.

rejected the Warren-Brandeis position cited above. Miller goes on to record that the New York legislature, on the court's suggestion, then enacted a statute making the use of personal information for such purposes a tort. As Miller notes, extension of this principle has since followed, although slowly and unevenly, in other states.[2]

Another twentieth-century privacy issue was that surrounding wiretapping and surreptitious recording, practices which first came into wide use in the 1920s. An examination of the entries under the heading "wiretapping" in the *New York Times Annual Index* shows publicity over the topic peaking just prior to the outbreak of World War II. Concern in these cases, however, seems rarely to have reflected disapproval of official wiretapping. Rather, the courts seemed to accord a certain legitimacy to such activities, while condemning private use of the practice. Alan Westin, for example, reports that during this time "there . . . [were] *no* convictions of police listeners under these statutes, despite the well-publicized wiretapping activities of policemen across the country."[3] The conflicts over these practices were to sharpen in the late 1960s and early 1970s.

Perhaps the most remarkable thing about the privacy issue as a whole before the 1960s was the seeming lack of one. Although there were disputes over many aspects of the handling of personal information, there seemed to be no public sensitivity to privacy in a global sense. Thus the linking, let us say, of controversies over polygraph testing with those over the confidentiality of government data files, as people seem to do today, did not exist in the 1950s. Indeed, computerized and other treatments of personal-data files were rarely a subject of public debate before the 1960s.

During the 1960s, many prerogatives of established organizations and groups which had gone unquestioned during the preceding decade became points of sharp contest. So it was in

[2] Quoted in ibid., p. 172. In New York the principle was established by statute after being rejected by the courts. In most other states, by contrast, the Warren-Brandeis principle was affirmed through judicial rather than through legislative action. We are grateful to Prof. Charles Marson of Stanford University Law School for clarifying this issue for us.

[3] Alan F. Westin, *Privacy and Freedom*. (New York: Atheneum, 1967), p. 178.

matters of privacy in general, and matters of surveillance in particular. In the late 1950s, a few stirrings were heard, most notably from intellectuals. In 1958–59, *The American Scholar* ran a series of articles under the heading "The Invasion of Privacy."[4] The first and the most impressive of these was by Richard Rovere, entitled "Technology and the Claims of Community."[5] Anticipating many later writings, he identified an overall crisis of privacy on a wide variety of fronts. Rovere sees social as well as technological origins to this state of affairs. He writes,

> My behavior affects my neighbor in a hundred ways undreamed of a century ago. My home is joined to his by pipes and cables, by tax and insurance rates. If my labor is not immediately dependent on his, it is on that of other men down the street and across the continent. When I move about, my life is at my neighbor's mercy—and his, of course, at mine. I may build a high fence, bolt the doors, draw the blinds and insist that my time to myself is mine alone, but his devices for intrusion are limitless. . . .
>
> The meaningful invasions that are a consequence of the condition of our lives are, to be sure, those undertaken more or less in the name of the whole community: by organs of government other than the police, by the press, by education, by business. Against them, the law can offer few defenses without denying other freedoms and committing new invasions of privacy.[6]

Of special import in the fusion of privacy into a coherent issue were two books published in 1964, *The Naked Society* by Vance Packard, and *The Privacy Invaders* by Myron Brenton.[7] Directed at a wider public than Rovere's article in *The American Scholar*, these two works, resembled it in treat-

[4] See *American Scholar*, Vols. 27 (Autumn 1958); 28 (Winter 1958–59); 28 (Spring 1959); 28 (Autumn 1959); 29 (Spring 1960).

[5] Richard H. Rovere, "The Invasion of Privacy (1): Technology and the Claims of Community," *American Scholar*, Vol. 27 (Autumn 1958), pp. 413–21.

[6] Ibid., pp. 419–20.

[7] Vance Packard, *The Naked Society* (New York: McKay, 1964); Myron Brenton, *The Privacy Invaders* (New York: Coward-McCann, 1964).

ing privacy as a global topic. In the deluge of writing on privacy since 1964, the considerable contribution of these books has largely been forgotten. Actually, both contain solid reportage on matters which, since then, have continued to draw considerable public comment. The books resemble each other in content, both dealing with credit, insurance, employment screening, polygraph testing, electronic snooping, mailing lists, and several other subjects. Government record-keeping on private persons was not much emphasized in either of these books, though both deal with privately run data systems such as those in credit and insurance. This is ironic in light of the special importance which government record-keeping was soon to assume in the emerging debates over privacy.

Beginning in 1965, privacy became a perennial subject of Congressional hearings and research. The extent of this activity is evident from the Appendix of the book, which is a selected listing of the major Congressional hearings and reports relating to privacy since that year.

As the Appendix shows, the earliest of these events were the hearings in 1965 by the Special Subcommittee on Invasion of Privacy of the House Government Operations Committee. These hearings touched on several forms of governmental information-gathering from private citizens, most notably personality testing. They produced the first blasts of what was to become standard privacy rhetoric. "All of us may one day stand psychologically naked," Congressman Gallagher of New Jersey declaimed; ". . . we have become a nation of snoopers."[8]

These hearings apparently brought some results. The Peace Corps, whose testing activities had been a central concern of the hearings, agreed to destroy existing test results and evaluations and not to require new applicants to take the tests in question.[9]

In 1965 and 1966, a subcommittee of the Senate Judiciary

[8] U.S. House of Representatives, *Special Inquiry on Invasions of Privacy,* Hearings before the Special Subcommittee on Invasion of Privacy of the Committee on Government Operations, House of Representatives, 89th Congress, 1st Session (Washington, D.C.: U.S. Government Printing Office, 1965), pp. 2–3.

[9] Ibid., pp. 238–41.

Committee held further hearings, later published under the title "Invasions of Privacy." These dealt with electronic surveillance, surveillance of Post Office employees, and "mail covers."[10]

Mail covers are the term for monitoring and recording by Post Office staff of the origins of mail addressed to given persons. Such practices are not illegal, nor is a warrant required before they can be placed. Testimony before the Senate subcommittee brought out that some 24,000 persons had been subjected to such surveillance in the preceding two years. In addition, it developed that postal officials had been systematically opening mail suspected of being "communist propaganda." Following the hearings, the Postmaster General announced new regulations limiting the authority to order mail covers, formerly held by all postmasters, to chief and regional postal inspectors. Law-enforcement agencies were required to submit requests for mail covers in writing.

These same hearings also came to involve the IRS, which, it was revealed, had used extensive electronic snooping measures to investigate suspected tax evaders. IRS Commissioner Sheldon Cohen and Attorney General Nicholas Katzenbach acknowledged such use, but contended that it was directed against organized crime, not ordinary taxpayers. Cohen claimed to have placed an unconditional ban on further wiretapping two weeks before the hearings, and Katzenbach emphasized the "isolated" nature of the activity, which in any event he purported to oppose, except for national-security cases.[11]

Perhaps the most significant hearings during this period were those held in 1966 and 1967 dealing with the proposed National Data Center.[12] The idea of such a center, which had

[10] U.S. Senate, *Invasions of Privacy,* Hearings before the Subcommittee on Administrative Practice and Procedure of the Committee on the Judiciary, United States Senate, 89th Congress, 1st Session (Washington, D.C.: U.S. Government Printing Office, 1965).

[11] Ibid., pp. 1124–29, 1155–61.

[12] U.S. House of Representatives, *The Computer and the Invasion of Privacy,* Hearings before the Special Subcommittee on Invasion of Privacy of the Committee on Government Operations, House of Representatives, 89th Congress, 2nd Session (Washington, D.C.: U.S. Government Printing Office, 1966); U.S Congress, *The Coordination and Integration of Government Statistical Programs,* Hearings before the Subcommittee on Economic Statistics of the Joint Economic Com-

arisen in social-science circles in the early '60s, was to gather in a single location personal information on Americans held by various federal agencies. Both private researchers and government planners had been frustrated by the difficulty of linking information held by the Census, for example, with that kept by the IRS, Social Security Administration, and other agencies. A preliminary study had identified some 600 different repositories of such information throughout the federal government. The planned linkage, which had its official support in the Bureau of the Budget, would bring these disparate elements together. Although data would be held in individually identifiable form, its purpose was to be limited to aggregate analysis; that is, it was not to be used for individual decision-making on the persons concerned.[13]

But the linkage of disparate strands of personal data, so appealing to the proponents, was repulsive to many others. Although plans for a National Data Center were never officially submitted to Congress, Senators and Representatives took the initiative to hold hearings on the matter. Representative Frank Horton of New York stated,

> Good computermen know that one of the most practical of our present safeguards of privacy is the fragmented nature of present information. It is scattered in little bits and pieces across the geography and years of our life. Retrieval is impractical and often impossible. A central data bank removes completely this safeguard.[14]

Proponents of the Data Center insisted that planners could devise effective safeguards for data which it might assemble. They contested the notion that dispersion of data guaranteed confidentiality and privacy. They stressed the distinction be-

---

mittee, 90th Congress, 1st Session (Washington, D.C.: U.S. Government Printing Office, 1967); U.S. Senate, *Computer Privacy*, Hearings before the Subcommittee on Administrative Practice and Procedure of the Committee on the Judiciary, United States Senate, 90th Congress, 1st Session (Washington, D.C.: U.S. Government Printing Office, 1967).

[13] For instance, see the testimony of Dr. Edgar Dunn, an economist who prepared an early report on the National Data Center for the Bureau of the Budget, in U.S. House of Representatives, *Computer and the Invasion of Privacy*, pp. 92–102.

[14] Ibid., p. 6.

tween statistical and intelligence uses of data, and insisted that the center was to remain strictly statistical. But their protestations met with skepticism from Representatives and Senators.

A more concrete proposal for a National Data Center never materialized. Apparently administration forces simply tested the political waters and found them too troubled to proceed. The effectiveness of opposition to the National Data Center demonstrated that public anxieties about bureaucratic use of personal data had developed a weighty political significance by the late 1960s.

A major focus of concern in the books by Brenton and Packard had been the activities of consumer-credit and insurance-reporting firms. In 1968 a subcommittee of the House Government Operations Committee held hearings first on credit, then on insurance surveillance. These hearings began a process which led, two years later, to passage of the Fair Credit Reporting Act. Professor Alan Westin, no doubt the most influential figure in the unfolding of the entire privacy issue, set the tone for the hearings as follows:

> Whenever any private activity becomes huge in size and financial resources, operates on a national scale, and affects the vital personal interests and civil liberties of millions of American citizens, such activity will come under Federal scrutiny and intervention to protect such citizen rights, especially when there is a vacuum of State and local legislation and court doctrines and an absence of decisive self-regulation within the industry.[15]

The response to this overture of the industry representatives who testified was mixed. H.C. Jordan, head of the innovative computerized Credit Data Corporation, made a favorable impression with the subcommittee by welcoming certain regulatory legislation; he also assured the members that his firm did not honor requests for personal data from government investigators without a subpoena. John Spafford, representing the conventional and more conservative arm of the industry, fared less well when he affirmed that firms repre-

[15] U.S. Congress, House Committee on Government Operations, *Commercial Credit Bureaus*, 90th Congress, 2nd Session, 12–14 March 1968 (Washington, D.C.: U.S. Government Printing Office, 1968), p. 4.

sented by him shared data freely with organizations such as the IRS and FBI, often at a financial loss. Representatives Gallagher and Rosenthal did not look at all favorably on this. The result was the following exchange:

> Mr. Gallagher. I would personally hope that you would stop serving the IRS. This insinuates a too friendly and cavalier exchange of information between you and the Government at the expense of the hapless American citizen. I like Dr. Jordan's approach. The whole issue perhaps should be one to be resolved by the courts. If it is one of issuing a subpena (sic), or a case of national security, I don't think anyone would object.
> Mr. Spafford. Wouldn't this increase the cost of Government operations considerably, sir?
> Mr. Gallagher. It may well, but I think a little extra cost in Government operations to prolong the civil liberties of people and their constitutional rights is a good investment.[16]

The tentative *prises de position* regarding the privacy issue by various participants in these hearings are important. At a number of points, the transcript shows Congressman Gallagher making rather strong statements, only to meet with more temperate remarks from Professor Westin. For example, the former remarked,

> The thing that disturbs me is that almost every human transaction must now be recorded with the Social Security number. It may be required everywhere. Into a Howard Johnson restroom, for example. Someone will probably justify the need for a Social Security number for entrance.
>
> If the peg of the Social Security number becomes the chief key in a national data bank—and incidentally the Census now wants to include your Social Security number—I have my doubts as to the number of options that the public may have in the future. . . . there are tendencies, corrosive tendencies on what people might view

[16] Ibid., p. 137.

> as their rights or liberties in one generation that no longer exists in the next.

To which Westin replied,

> That is a very important point. Over the decades, people's conceptions change as to what part of them is private and what they are revealing that troubles them.

And a bit later, Professor Westin continued,

> . . . by and large, Americans are changing their conceptions of what is private. I'm not really trying to say this is good or bad. . . . If something becomes so widespread that the great majority of the public says this doesn't worry us so much, then that changes the definition of the relation between private and public.[17]

Following the 1968 hearings, legislation which was to become the Fair Credit Reporting Act was introduced into the Senate. On November 5, 1969, after favorable committee action, the upper house passed the measure by a voice vote. The House Banking and Currency Subcommittee on Consumer Affairs held its hearings on credit-reporting practices, which included consideration of the Senate-passed bill, in March and April of 1970. A House-Senate conference committee ironed out differences between the two bodies on the legislation in October, and Senate and House agreed to the conference report by voice vote. President Nixon signed the bill into law on October 26, 1970. The details of the Fair Credit Reporting Act are discussed at length in the following chapter.

As these events were unfolding within the specialized world of consumer credit, more convulsive changes were taking place in American public life. These were the years of the Vietnam War, and of all the associated tensions between those in power and political dissenters of all kinds. Virtually at the height of these tensions, newspapers carried stories that the Army had been maintaining surveillance over domestic pro-

[17] Ibid., pp. 55–56.

test and protestors. In Illinois alone, it was charged, some 800 people had been targeted for military surveillance; these apparently included not only political dissidents but also major elected officials.

What caused even more outcry was the revelation that the Army investigations fed into a vast, computerized network maintained throughout the country and centrally orchestrated. According to one report,

> The Defense Central Index of Investigations at Ft. Holabird, Maryland, which "serves as the central index—the key—to the counterintelligence and criminal investigative files of the Department of Defense," has about 25,-000,000 index cards on persons and 760,000 on organizations and incidents. A daily average of 12,000 requests are processed, and 20,000 additions, deletions and changes are made. . . . By July 1971, the index will be completely punch-carded for computerized searches.
>
> The Army's Investigative Records Repository at Ft. Holabird has 7,890,630 files on persons and organizations. The Navy maintains about 3,000,000 investigative files and the Air Force 2,581,618.[18]

The tone of Senatorial response to these activities was set by Senator Ervin, chairman of the subcommittee, on the first day of the hearings:

> Full-scale dossiers on thousands of Americans, compendiums, blacklists, computer systems, city books, and massive surveillance by the U.S. Army Intelligence Command and the other military services clearly amount to a clear and present danger to First Amendment freedom.[19]

Most of those who appeared before the subcommittee were critical of the military surveillance. These included a wide range of witnesses, from political officeholders to figures from groups such as the American Friends Service Committee; there were also people from universities and private

[18] Congressional Quarterly, *Almanac, 92nd Congress, 1st Session, 1971* (Washington, D.C.: Congressional Quarterly, 1972, pp. 775–76.
[19] Ibid., p. 774.

business. Reading through these remarks, one is struck by the extent to which consciousness of bureaucratic surveillance had permeated public thinking. For example, note the testimony of Jerome Wiesner, then president-elect of the Massachusetts Institute of Technology:

> I doubt that anyone is aware of the full extent of the surveillance and information-collection activities that go on in this nation. Many people, myself included, have long operated on the assumption that our activities are being monitored.

Then Wiesner concluded with a sweeping suggestion:

> We should be prepared to accept the cost of considerable inefficiency in our various social and governmental processes to safeguard our privacy, and, as I judge it, our freedom, dignity, happiness and self-respect. By costs, I mean both the financial costs and the loss of a degree of control that the state might otherwise have over genuinely threatening individuals. . . .[20]

On the other side of the controversy, administration officials entered vigorous defenses of government surveillance activities. Robert Froehlke, Assistant Secretary of Defense, denied any wrongdoing:

> Since no use of civil disturbance information was made or intended to be made that would result in any action to the persons involved, we cannot perceive how the constitutional rights or even the right of privacy could be impinged by the collection of such information.[21]

Froehlke went on to reveal that the White House and Justice Department had participated in planning military surveillance.

The results of these hearings were indecisive. The controversy apparently prompted the Army to tighten somewhat its

[20] Ibid., p. 777.
[21] Ibid., p. 775.

directives governing civilian surveillance. But the hearings ended without any more far-reaching commitment to curtail these activities.

The 1970s continued to produce one bumper crop after another of Congressional hearings and reports relating to privacy. Most of these dealt with subjects already touched upon by Congressional inquiries in the late 1960s—psychological testing, the Census, law-enforcement surveillance, etc. If there is any trend at all in the subject matter of these concerns, it seems to lie in the direction of increasing focus on data files and dossiers, in relation to other privacy-related issues.

Of course, none of these subtler trends rivals the dominant political events of those times in shaping the status of privacy as a public issue. The Watergate drama, with its many twists and subplots, did perhaps more than anything else to force official treatment of personal data into the arena of public controversy. Every element of the scandals seemed to involve some conflict over official use of personal data—bugging, snooping into psychiatric records, misuse of the surveillance capacities of agencies like the IRS, or whatever. By 1973, it was apparent that privacy was an issue to be reckoned with—in Congress and across the land.

Coincidentally or not, 1973 saw the appearance of *Records, Computers and the Rights of Citizens*, a report published by the Department of Health, Education and Welfare. Commissioned by Elliot Richardson during his tenure as HEW Secretary, the report reviewed the changes in personal record-keeping wrought by the advent of the computer, and suggested policy responses to these changes. Such a report would no doubt have drawn much attention even under ordinary circumstances. But its juxtaposition to the Watergate affair greatly multiplied its impact. The viewpoint developed in this study receives detailed attention in the following chapter.

By early 1974, of course, the Watergate crisis was reaching its climax. The Nixon administration evidently concluded that it could no longer afford to be on the losing end of the privacy issue. Thus there occurred, on February 23 of that year, one of the more ironic events of a period rich in political ironies: Richard Nixon's nationwide radio address, "The American Right to Privacy." "Here is the heart of the matter," the President stated:

> What a person earns, what he owes, what he gives to his church or to his charity is his own personal business and should not be spread around without his consent. When personal information is given or obtained for one purpose such as a loan or credit at a store, it should not be secretly used by anyone for any other purpose.

Mr. Nixon went on to announce the establishment of the Domestic Council Committee on the Right of Privacy, headed by the Vice-President and composed of cabinet members and other high officials. This was to be an "action group," charged with pursuing privacy issues as they arose within the federal government. The activities of the Committee staff were to have an important role in the passage of some of the legislation discussed below.

In Congress, meanwhile, the same sentiments which were to bring the Nixon administration to an end were providing the impetus for the Privacy Act of 1974. Introduced separately in House and Senate, both versions of the legislation required controls on the collection and use of personal data by state and federal agencies and certain private organizations. In addition, the Senate version, introduced by Sam Ervin of North Carolina, embodied plans for a permanent Privacy Protection Commission, to monitor federal data systems.

The Ford administration made numerous objections to both bills, opposing, for example, the Privacy Commission idea and the provisions of the bills dealing with state and private organizations. These efforts, mainly directed at the stronger Senate version, were successful at a number of points, as the limitations written into the Privacy Act attest. Nonetheless, the climate of the times made it impossible to muster the opposition necessary to block the legislation outright. The Senate version passed by a vote of 74 to 9, and the House version by a vote of 353 to 1. Final passage came on December 18. Provisions of the act are discussed in detail in Part II.

It is interesting to note the voting patterns associated with the Privacy Act. Voting on the act itself was too lopsided to afford many significant comparisons, but the vote on one of the key attempts to weaken the act through amendment presents some more interesting contrasts. This is the Erlenborn amendment, ultimately passed by the House by a vote of 192 to 177. It was supported overwhelmingly by Republicans and opposed by a wide majority of Democrats. A close look at the records of those voting on the amendment reveals that the support for it was directly associated with high ratings by conservative legislative watchdog organizations, such as Americans for Constitutional Action and the National Association of Businessmen, and opposition to it was associated with high ratings from the liberal counterparts of these organizations, such as Americans for Democratic Action, the AFL-CIO Committee on Political Education, and the Consumer Federation of America. Thus friendliness to the purposes of the Privacy Act seems generally associated with the broad dimension of Congressional liberalism.

During the height of the Watergate period, no one dared to oppose privacy overtly—although, as we argue in the following chapter, the principle enjoyed some strange forms of "support." One example was a remarkable event in the House of Representatives on April 2, 1974. Christened a "Congressional Commitment to Privacy" by its sponsors, the occasion consisted simply of an opportunity for Representatives to expound for the public record in favor of privacy. At least sixty availed themselves of the opportunity, often taking the chance to recall some early speech or other evidence of being *bona fide* on the subject.

The 1976 hearings of the Senate-House Subcommittee on Administration of the Internal Revenue Code dealing with tax return confidentiality were another event of the Watergate period. News stories asserted that the Nixon administration had exploited IRS data and enforcement capabilities as means of harassing White House enemies. Related practices had apparently taken place well before the Nixon years, but reached some sort of culmination then. Apparently the White House, between 1969 and 1973, had applied pressure on the IRS to act against political enemies of the administration. These enemies included not only extremists but also mainstream figures such as Lawrence O'Brien. The White House succeeded in bypassing usual IRS procedures and obtaining IRS data on such persons; it then funneled the information to those likely to use it against the persons concerned, including in at least one case the CIA.[22] An early IRS memo on the subject noted, "From a strictly revenue standpoint, we may have little reason for establishing [these operations] . . . or for expending the time and effort which may be necessary." Nevertheless, the memo continued, "we must do it."[23]

Again, while the dominant tone of these hearings was indignation at the practices being uncovered, the results remained less than sweeping. Senator Weicker of Connecticut stated at one point that the country had had enough of "bombshells" and "horror stories" and chided the Congress for not taking concrete action to end Watergate-like abuses. "The danger in this country today is no longer suppression of the truth," he noted, "but the willingness to live with that portion of the truth which runs counter to American concepts of justice and confidentiality."

These Congressional activities were but one indication of the growing national concern over organizational treatment of personal data. These events are important, since they led more or less directly to the formulation of official privacy policy. But even if this Congressional activity had not taken place, there would still have been ample evidence for the growing public salience of the privacy issue.

The results of public-opinion polls illustrate the same point, although we have much less of this kind of evidence than that from the *Congressional Record*. For example, in a nationally representative sampling of some 2,000 adults conducted in 1970, respondents were asked to indicate which of an array of subjects people had "heard or read most about in recent months." Some 23 percent cited "invasion of privacy," while 33 percent cited "wiretapping or bugging of a telephone by a government investigative agency." By comparison, the figures were 65 percent for "high automobile insurance rates" and 44 percent for "low quality education in the public schools." Re-

[22] Reported in Jerry J. Berman and Morton Halpern, eds., "The Abuses of the Intelligence Agencies," entered into the record as part of the testimony of Mrs. Hope Eastman of the American Civil Liberties Union, U.S. Senate, *Federal Tax Return Privacy*, hearing before the Committee on Finance Subcommittee on Administration of the Internal Revenue Code. 94th Congress, 2nd Session, 23 January 1976 (Washington, D.C.: U.S. Government Printing Office, 1976), p. 13.

[23] Ibid., p. 14.

sponses to similar queries two years later remained within a few percentage points of these same figures.[24]

Another indication of public sentiment from the same year came in a study by David Armor and associates. In a survey of some 201 respondents from three socially heterogeneous Massachusetts communities, the researchers asked the following question, which obviously referred to the National Data Center controversy:

> As you know, the government now collects different kinds of information on people, such as income tax, census, Social Security records, criminal records, and military records. There has been some talk of the government using computers to establish a national databank—a computerized file which would combine all of this information in one place. Those proposing this see it as a way of increasing efficiency; critics say that it would be an invasion of privacy. Would you personally favor or oppose such a development?

Fifty-six percent of the respondents classified themselves as opposed, 31 percent as supportive, with the remainder undecided.[25] If these figures are representative of national trends at the time, they suggest that the opponents of the Data Center idea were shrewd in invoking privacy objections to it.

There can be little question of the authenticity of public concerns over privacy. On the other hand, Americans' beliefs seem to be diffuse and indeed contradictory on the implications of these privacy concerns for action. In the first, larger poll mentioned above, some 94 percent of the respondents in 1970 concurred that a credit grantor "has a right to investigate [the borrower] as to his ability to meet payments."[26] Yet in the Armor study, 60 percent of the respondents held that it was wrong for credit bureaus "to have a lot of information

[24] The results of these two surveys are presented in an untitled release from the Retail Credit Company (now Equifax), dated November 1972, p. 2.

[25] Cited in Alan F. Westin and Michael Baker, *Databanks in a Free Society* (New York: Quadrangle/The New York Times Book Co., 1972), p. 470.

[26] Retail Credit Company, 1972, p. 5.

about people's finances."[27] Similar contradictions emerged in a national survey conducted in 1971 by the American Federation of Information Processing Societies and *Time* magazine. Of the 1,001 adults questioned, 75 percent believed that "computers will improve our lives" in the future. At the same time, however, 58 percent felt that "computers will be used to keep people under surveillance."[28]

Perhaps the one clear trend which emerges from the available public-opinion data is that of growing suspicion and uneasiness about personal data files and their consequences. Given the march of national events reflected in Congressional hearings and reports, this trend should not come as a surprise. The following findings are drawn from a national Harris poll in which the same questions were posed to different, but representative, selections of respondents in 1974, 1976, and 1977, and 1978:[29] "Some people say that Americans begin surrendering their privacy the day they open their first charge account, take out a loan, buy something on the installment plan or apply for a credit card. All in all, do you tend to agree or disagree with this statement?"

	1974	1976	1977	1978
Agree	48%	47%	67%	76%
Disagree	43%	47%	24%	21%
Not sure	9%	6%	9%	3%

"Do you believe that personal information about yourself is being kept in some files somewhere for purposes not known to you, or don't you believe this is so?"

(continued)

[27] Westin and Baker, *Databank in a Free Society*, p. 470.

[28] American Federation of Information Processing Societies and *Time* magazine, *A National Survey of the Public's Attitudes Towards Computers* (New York: Time, Inc., 1973), table 25.

[29] The first set of figures is from Louis Harris and Associates, "The Dimensions of Privacy, p. 20 (New York: 1979). The second two sets are from "Our Privacy in Danger" (Chicago: The Chicago Tribune Co.: 1977).

	1974	1976	1977
Believe	44%	48%	54%
Don't believe	44%	43%	32%
Not sure	12%	9%	14%

"Do you feel threatened in any way by having information about yourself in some files, or don't you feel threatened by that?"

	1974	1976	1977
Feel threatened	23%	27%	32%
Don't	75%	69%	62%
Not sure	2%	4%	6%

According to these figures, a growing number of people feel threatened by data files on themselves. And the findings of the Congressional inquiries suggest that such feelings may be eminently reasonable. By the late 1960s, the use of personal-data files by both public and private bureaucracies had come under attack, and both sides seem to have understood that the contest was about something important. But it remained unclear precisely what changes in organizational practice the critics would demand.

PART II

The Official Response

By the late 1960s, ability to collect, store, and use personal information had become a major resource for key American bureaucracies, both public and private. Yet some of the popular objections to these practices sounded serious indeed. Given rising public mistrust of established institutions—culminating, ultimately, in the Watergate affair—the nascent "privacy protection movement" of the late 1960s might have led to fundamental attacks upon established power positions.

But in fact, no frontal collision has occurred between an aroused public opinion and organizations engaged in what we term surveillance. The emergent official interpretation of "privacy protection" has forestalled any such confrontation. In this view, the drawbacks of surveillance systems are not inherent in their nature, but lie in their failure to work "correctly." And "correctly," in this context, means "efficiently" from the standpoint of the long-term interests of the organization. This convenient assumption has made it possible to pursue the "reform" of surveillance practices in ways which enhance, rather than threaten, bureaucratic interests.

The defusing of the privacy issue has many parallels in the history of American attempts to regulate noxious practices by powerful institutions. In the case of privacy, as with many other issues, the fateful turning point came not in the heat of public debate, but at the unnoticed point where key assumptions were taken for granted.

Of special importance in shaping these assumptions during the early years of debate on privacy was the tendency to focus on certain notorious "abuses" of personal-data practices. Congressional hearings, journalistic and popular writings, and scholarly treatments of the emergent issue all tended to dramatize certain categories of particularly ugly misuses of personal information. They publicized cases where credit bureaus caused damage by maintaining and reporting erroneous information. Or they focused on instances where erroneous or misleading arrest data unjustly affected people's access to employment. Or they centered attention on cases where an early education record unfairly stigmatized a child throughout his school career.

Such abuses are easy targets, since they represent cases where surveillance systems both frustrate the interests of individuals and hinder the larger interests of the organization. Not only do innocent parties find their access to credit unfairly blocked, but credit-granting institutions also lose potentially valuable customers. Not only does a schoolchild suffer from others' false assumptions about his or her abilities or personality, but the school loses the opportunity it might have had for more effective teaching based on more accurate information. Sequences like these proved easy to attack, since no one wanted to defend them.

Those in charge of surveillance systems showed two kinds of response to the revelation of such abuses. The more conservative—and less imaginative—of these responses was simply to deny the charges—to label the abuses unrepresentative, to insist that procedures already established could correct them, or simply to maintain that personal-data management is the legitimate concern only of the managers. Another response, however, was much shrewder. This was to accept critics' objections and the legitimacy of efforts to correct abuses. In so doing, however, the defenders of surveillance helped shift the debate over "privacy protection" to one over elimination of particular sets of abusive practices. And this was construed to mean making surveillance systems work better—with the assumption that both organizations and individuals shared an interest in their enhanced efficiency. By concentrating on abuses of personal record-keeping so ex-

treme that they served neither individuals nor organizations, the larger questions were deftly obscured: How much surveillance do we really want? How far into previously private areas of life ought these systems to extend? At what point does even just, efficient monitoring of private affairs become excessive?

Instead of confronting these enormously difficult and far-reaching questions, however, the planners eventually evolved what we term "the efficiency criterion" for the protection of privacy in personal-data systems. By this criterion, surveillance is considered acceptable provided that four conditions are met: first, that personal data are kept accurate, complete, and up to date; second, that openly promulgated rules of "due process" govern the workings of data systems, including the decision-making based on the data; third, that organizations collect and use personal data only as necessary to attain "legitimate" organizational goals; fourth, that the people described in data files have the right to monitor and contest adherence to these principles. By these criteria, organizations can claim to protect the privacy of those with whom they deal, even as they demand more and more data from them and accumulate ever more power over their lives. From the standpoint of surveillance organizations, this is a most opportune interpretation of "privacy protection."

But the terms of this emergent compromise neglect something very important. The growth of modern bureaucratic surveillance represents a social trend of enormous significance in itself. That significance lies, above all, in the changes wrought by personal-data systems in fundamental social relationships, above all power relationships. These changes pose issues much more profound than those addressed by "reform" of systems so as to prevent "abuses" like those discussed above.

We perceive excellent reasons to beware of the unlimited growth of bureaucratic surveillance, even when free of immediate "abuses." For the growth of these systems threatens to centralize power over people's lives to an undesirable extent, to undermine what we have termed "aesthetic" satisfactions in keeping private spheres private, and to render social systems excessively "unforgiving" in their effects on individuals. Intelligent planning could well identify attractive alternatives to reliance on more and more intense surveil-

lance. Yet these less "information-intensive" alternatives—as we call procedures which demand less information from people, yet produce comparable services—have received little attention in the official response to the privacy issue.

The beguiling thing about the emergent reform consensus is that it seems to offer something for everybody. For the general public, beset by demands for personal data, it offers assurance that "privacy" is being "protected," even as organizations amass more and more personal information. Yet such protection is to be achieved without disturbing any of the conveniences associated in the public mind with organizational surveillance. From the institutional point of view, the picture is even brighter. In exchange for acceptance of procedural reforms, surveillance organizations achieve legitimacy and public support for their activities.

Perhaps most important of all, acceptance of the "efficiency criterion" undercuts potential public opposition to more and more sweeping surveillance: It becomes impossible to object to any *surveillance practice, provided that data are used efficiently for the ends of some established organization—and provided this use occurs with fairness, accuracy, thoroughness, due process, and provision for participation by the individual concerned. Having agreed to play the game, those speaking for the interests of the public can hardly complain as the stakes are raised. And these stakes, in terms of the shifting balance of power between mass publics and centralized organizations, may well rise without limit. Thus the official interpretation of privacy protection actually encourages the growth of surveillance and the erosion of personal privacy.*

But we are getting ahead of ourselves. We must trace the intellectual and political evolution of these questionable compromises, and consider their context in American life. Then we can explore some of the wider social choices which the official positions threaten to dismiss.

7 □ Alan Westin: Privacy and Freedom (1967)

Westin's work in general, and *Privacy and Freedom* in particular, have shaped virtually all current thinking about privacy as a public issue.[1] Indeed, other than Ralph Nader, no figure comes to mind who has so decisively shaped the public view of any current issue. *Privacy and Freedom* appeared just as the issue was intruding itself into the national consciousness. More than previous statements, however, this book offered a comprehensive, scholarly interpretation of privacy, coupled with a detailed and well articulated agenda for action.

Privacy and Freedom is, first, a big book; nearly 400 dense pages. Those pages present a wealth of research, mainly the results of gleanings from newspapers and general publications, but also syntheses of wide readings in the social sciences, law, and other areas. The book is divided into four parts. The first deals with the nature of privacy and its past and present role in social and legal thought. The second section details the encroachments on personal privacy brought about by modern data-management practices. The third section presents five case studies of policy-making in matters relating to privacy—electronic surveillance, polygraph testing, personality testing, subliminal advertising, and the manipulation of personal-data files. The final section appraises the

[1] Alan F. Westin, *Privacy and Freedom* (New York: Atheneum, 1967).

state of law and policy on privacy and offers suggestions for further change. After ten years, much of the *reportage* of the book does not strike one as remarkable. Revelations about such things as hidden microphones have been so thoroughly assimilated that they no longer astound us. The underlying structure of Westin's argument and his policy conclusions, however, have continued to exert enormous influence over subsequent discussion and action.

The sociological analysis which underlies the work is not complex. Westin sees the "privacy problem" as arising from intrusion into previously "balanced" social relationships. The intrusive force is technology, which has created all sorts of pressures against privacy not anticipated in the privacy-protecting conventions of previous periods. In the "imbalanced" state which has resulted, people are at least potentially less protected than before against these pressures. But nothing about the present imbalance is irremediable. The updating of legislation and policy to render it consistent with present realities should, to use an oft-repeated phrase in all these discussions, "restore the balance." Basically this is the logic of the "cultural lag," as originally enunciated by Ogburn.[2] In this view, all sorts of "social problems" are seen to stem from the need for updating social practice to accord with new social realities.

Perhaps the most valuable aspect of Westin's analysis is his historical exposition of privacy issues in Anglo-American legal and social thought. Far from being an altogether new concern, Westin argues, the desire to restrict access to personal information was a key influence in the framing of the American Constitution. Thus he writes,

> The technological realities of eighteenth- and early nineteenth-century America limited communication to direct speech or letter. Eyes and ears were the only instruments for physical surveillance; penetration of the mind was possible only by torture or compelled testimony; and there was little extensive record keeping about individuals. Given this setting, American constitutional, statutory, and common law concentrated on establishing

[2] William Fielding Ogburn, *On Culture and Social Change: Selected Papers*, ed. by Otis Dudley Duncan (Chicago: University of Chicago Press, 1964), pp. 86–95.

> shields of privacy to protect individual and organizational autonomy, ensure personal and family privacy in the home, and safeguard confidentiality in the basic modes of communication.[3]

These observations give force to his arguments on the disruptive role of new technologies in making personal data more easily available. Thus remedial action is required to "redress the balance" impaired through these changes.

Westin relies heavily on this "balancing" language. In introducing his recommendations for policy, for example, he writes,

> If privacy is to receive its proper weight on the scales in any process of balancing competing values what is needed is a structured and rational weighing process with definite criteria that public and private authorities can apply in comparing the claims for disclosure or surveillance through new devices with the claims to privacy.[4]

To this end, he suggests five broad questions the answers to which ought, in his view, to guide reform of personal-data management. First, is the need for this form of personal information really serious enough to warrant its collection? Second, may there not be alternate methods of meeting the need? Third, is the form of inquiry reliable; that is, does it really allow the judgments which the situation requires? Fourth, what form of consent, if any, do the individuals concerned offer to the collection of the information? Finally, how trustworthy is the agency which administers the information-gathering?

Westin feels that queries along these lines can lead to restraints at a number of points.[5] These include enhanced public consciousness of the issues; scientific countermeasures to foil surveillance technologies; policy decisions within organizations to forego privacy-invading practices; agreements among organizations, e.g., collective-bargaining agreements to limit surveillance in the workplace; and the adoption of pri-

[3] Westin, *Privacy and Freedom*, p. 330.
[4] Ibid., p. 370.
[5] Ibid., pp. 380–99.

vacy-protecting standards by professional bodies. A second major category of recommendations has to do with government action. Here Westin's recommendations run through a wide range of possibilities: outright curtailment of certain practices, like most forms of polygraph examination; the creation of government regulatory bodies; the close regulation of such things as wiretapping; and, finally, legislation to control the treatment of personal-data files. Since the appearance of *Privacy and Freedom,* nearly all of these measures have been either implemented or actively discussed in official contexts.

Some of the recommendations put forward in *Privacy and Freedom* have had especially far-reaching effects on subsequent legislation. For example, he argues for a "property" model for personal information, which he explains as follows:

> With personal information so defined, a citizen would be entitled to have due process of law before his property could be taken and misused by government or by agencies exercising such enormous public power that they would be held to the same rules as government. Allowing for certain exceptions . . . an individual would have to be notified when information was put into key central files. He would be able, if he desired, to examine the information that had been put into his file, to challenge its accuracy in some kind of administrative proceeding (with court review), and to submit a reply or explanation that would be coupled permanently to the information.[6]

As the following pages show, this passage has provided a template for much official writing and legislation on the subject.

Privacy and Freedom is a deeply optimistic work. It combines grave warnings on the state of privacy with bright messages concerning the susceptibility of these shortcomings to redress. None of the conditions which Westin so articulately deplores does he consider beyond the reach of corrective action. The essence of the troubles, after all, is an

[6] Ibid., p. 325.

imbalance, something which can be compensated for by self-conscious action to bring current data-handling practices into line with current technological realities.

The notion of "redressing an imbalance" has a wholesome ring to it; it sounds like the sort of program which no one could possibly fault. But providing a "structured and rational weighing process," to use Westin's words, is a large order. When examined, the "balances" which he proposes to strike do not seem to be informed by any rigorous or consistently applied principle. Indeed, he does not take seriously enough the task of weighing the risks against benefits in modern personal-data practices.

Sometimes, for example, Westin finds certain practices so upsetting as to warrant their virtual eradication. The use of the lie detector, he feels, invades an "inner domain" of individual "belief, tendency and inclination"; it robs the individual of a valuable sense of autonomy, and establishes an unacceptable imbalance of power between the interests sponsoring the tests and the taker. On all these grounds, he argues, polygraph testing ought to be forbidden to government and private organizations except for a narrow range of national-security uses. He is nearly as sweeping in his skepticism of what he regards as especially intrusive forms of personality testing.[7] And these suggestions, if implemented, would indeed result in a form of "redress," if by that one means return to the situation like that which existed before these methods came into being.

But Westin finds nothing inherently worrisome about growth in the use of personal information by organizations; his concern is simply that these practices proceed according to acceptable procedural rules. The quote above on the "property" model for personal-data handling provides an excellent example of the procedural reforms which he favors. He does not believe it possible that extensive surveillance systems may give organizations too much power over individuals. Indeed, in a study published in 1971, he seems to accept as inevitable and desirable what he describes as

> the creation of more and more advanced types of computerized information systems with two basic principles

[7] Ibid., pp. 242–78.

> at their core: full *consolidation* of relevant data and full *circulation* of this data to all appropriate agencies.[8]

And he comments, on this point,

> Not to consolidate and circulate data would be to deny the essential logic and thrust of the technology. Such self-denial has often occurred in the very early stages of a new technology (for example, using the automobile as a horseless carriage), but it is not usually continued once the essence of the new technology has been realized.[9]

Westin acknowledges that these developments may well disturb persons subjected to such data-monitoring processes. But the grounds for these fears can be removed by regulation and reform. He writes,

> Whether computerized data systems *will* have these [undesirable] potential effects, however, is a question of social policy, not technology. It depends on how computer usage is shaped by the American political culture.[10]

For Westin, no form of institutional power is so great that it cannot be made acceptable through judicious monitoring. In another statement written at about the same time as *Privacy and Freedom,* Westin declares,

> The fact is that American society wants both better information analysis *and* privacy. Ever since the Constitution was written, our efforts to have both order and liberty have succeeded because we found ways to grant authority to government but to tie it down with the clear standards, operating procedures, and review mechanisms that protected individual rights. A free society should not have to choose between more rational use of author-

[8] Alan F. Westin, "Civil Liberties and Computerized Data Systems," in Martin Greenberger, ed., *Computers, Communications and the Public Interest* (Baltimore: Johns Hopkins, 1971), p. 157.
[9] Ibid.
[10] Ibid., p. 158.

> ity and personal privacy if our talents for democratic government are brought to bear on the task.[11]

Thus, an optimistic message indeed.

But this conclusion evades a searching assessment of the risks of large-scale surveillance. Why is Westin so optimistic about the susceptibility of personal-data systems to reform, while declaring the polygraph, for example, unacceptable? Perhaps because the polygraph invades an "inner domain," where the individual is most vulnerable. But while the experience of being subjected to bureaucratic demands for documentary information may be less dramatic than that of being subjected to the polygraph, the social consequences remain serious in both cases.

Westin overlooks the fundamental shift in prerogatives and power involved in the development of surveillance systems. By implying that the "wrongs" associated with these systems are simply matters of improper handling of particular individual cases, he fails to address the larger social effects of the systems.

These global effects are the most important of all. Even if all the procedural "abuses" of personal-data handling could be eliminated, vast problems would remain. The simplest of these is that most people simply do not like the idea of unlimited organizational monitoring of otherwise private affairs.[12] Curtailing the growth of surveillance, in other words, has an "aesthetic" value for most people. Moreover, the growth of bureaucratic surveillance inevitably enhances the potential for repressive control. Guided by procedural reforms or not, surveillance systems heighten the concrete and potential influence of centralized powers, both by what they accomplish and by what people fear that they may accomplish. A system of income-taxation surveillance, for example, can also monitor the activities of dissidents and provide means for their harassment. A consumer-credit-reporting sys-

[11] Alan F. Westin, "Civil Liberties Issues in Public Databanks," in Alan F. Westin, ed., *Information Technology in a Democracy* (Cambridge, Mass.: Harvard University Press, 1971), p. 310.

[12] Note, for example, the expressions of public disquiet, however vague and ambivalent, over the growth of personal record-keeping as discussed at the end of the preceding chapter.

tem can also provide data on the movements, resources, and consumption habits on those regarded as enemies by the interests in control of the systems. The result, should such risks materialize, is not only discrete "abuses" to individuals but also the poisoning of broad relationships between centralized institutions and the public.

"The effective use of computers calls for rational analysis and painstaking planning," Westin writes. "If privacy is to survive," he continues,

> the growth of personal-data processing will necessitate the same high level of analysis and planning. . . . Provisions for confidentiality of information, restrictions on improper circulation, and sanctions against unauthorized use should be written into the basic legislation and administrative rules. . . .[13]

These ideas, as the following pages will show, have been prophetic of the broad drift of national privacy-protection policy. But the author never seriously weighs the possibility that even systems set up under stringent procedural guarantees may eventually serve unacceptable purposes. His confidence in the strength of due-process guarantees is touching, but unexamined.

The hindsight afforded in the eleven years since publication of *Privacy and Freedom* sometimes places this confidence in an embarrassing light. In seeking rigorous adherence to privacy standards in law-enforcement, for example, he writes,

> . . . the history of police-force use of eavesdropping is sufficiently stained with misconduct throughout the nation that use of physical surveillance devices at the state level should be strictly limited to district attorneys' offices and state attorney generals' offices, and at the federal level to the FBI and military agencies.[14]

Clearly the logic of Westin's position requires that some agency or organization be considered sufficiently reliable to be entrusted to use surveillance wisely. But in light of events

[13] Westin, *Privacy and Freedom*, p. 386.
[14] Ibid., p. 376.

since 1967, the choice of the FBI and military intelligence for this role can only be described as quaint.

We endorse the importance of procedural guarantees of due process, administered by the most trustworthy agencies available, for any personal-data system whose existence is deemed essential. But such guarantees hardly eliminate the considerable social risks of such systems. The "rational analysis and painstaking planning" cited by Westin as essential should aim at minimizing reliance on personal-data systems, rather than at streamlining their growth. Not to seek such alternatives is to place ever more sweeping trust in the eternal discretion of human institutions; and such trust is better avoided in any world peopled by mortals.

Perhaps the crux of our dissatisfaction with Westin's position is his assumption that due-process guarantees establishing such things as "confidentiality of information, restrictions on improper circulation, and sanctions against unauthorized use" effectively "redress the balance" between individuals and centralized institutions. Certainly such guarantees, when they work, may establish limits to organizations' power. But such procedural limitations can scarcely recreate the distribution of power that existed before these centralized data systems grew up. Not to recognize the development of the federal income-taxation system or the consumer-credit-reporting system, in either regulated or unregulated form, as a clear-cut increase in power for centralized institutions is to ignore some fundamental realities of highly developed societies.

It is interesting to recall Westin's original definition of privacy, given at the beginning of *Privacy and Freedom*. Privacy, he writes, "is the claim of individuals, groups, or institutions to determine for themselves when, how, and to what extent information about them is communicated to others."[15] Although this definition has been widely used in subsequent privacy discussions, it surely does not correspond exactly with the way the term is used in everyday discourse. One would not say that a politician, an actress, or a self-dramatizing gossip enjoys privacy, for example. Such people systematically shed their privacy, in exchange for something: power, recognition, or wealth, for example. One does not pity them, since their renunciation of privacy is voluntary. But to

[15] Ibid., p. 7.

claim that they enjoy privacy in the same sense that a really self-effacing person enjoys it, simply because both types of people have exercised some control in the matter, seems to us to confuse two rather different conditions.

This aspect of Westin's definition has always puzzled us. But it is at least consistent with his subsequent arguments. For this definition makes it plausible to contend that "privacy" is "protected" in personal-data systems, if only people are accorded some say in the treatment of their information. But in a deeper sense, the demands of modern surveillance systems can only be destructive of what people ordinarily think of as privacy. Procedural guarantees may succeed in offering the individual some role in shaping the treatment of his or her data. But no one can live anything like a normal life in a modern, bureaucratic society without providing significant amounts of personal information to organizations. And no one ever has absolute control over the uses of such data by the organizations; if that were the case, the data would be useless to the organizations concerned. The growth of demands for personal information from modern organizations may to some extent be compensated for by the lessening of such demands from family and community. The costs of providing such information to organizations may, in given cases, be justified by overriding considerations of other goods. But it would be ridiculous to deny that the development of modern surveillance wears away at privacy in the sense that people ordinarily use that word.

8 □ Arthur R. Miller: The Assault on Privacy (1971)

The Assault on Privacy[1] focuses its attention more heavily on the treatment of data files by government and private organizations, the issue of greatest policy and legislative interest in the late 1960s and 1970s. Like Westin's *Privacy and Freedom,* Miller's book concludes with a detailed discussion of policy possibilities for the protection of privacy. These suggestions have had nearly as much impact on the course of subsequent discussion as have Westin's.

The Assault on Privacy opens with discussion of the scientific and technological changes which, in Miller's view, have given rise to the privacy issue. He then proceeds to more detailed examination of actual uses of personal information in psychological testing, consumer credit, the Census, and other areas. Another two sections of the book offer a history and a critique of the current legal status of privacy. The closing sections of the book give Miller's suggestions for "restoring the balance"—a phrase familiar to readers of Westin.

The earlier parts of the book are full of interesting anecdotes, but the underlying argument is weak. Miller argues, unexceptionably, that modern technologies have led to creation, transmission, and use of information, including per-

[1] Arthur R. Miller, *The Assault on Privacy* (Ann Arbor, Mich.: University of Michigan Press, 1971).

sonal information. Clearly Miller believes that these new possibilities have brought about all sorts of social mischief; indeed, the assumption seems to be virtually identical to Westin's view of technology as a disruptive force in relation to previously established social and legal "balances."[2] But Miller offers even less formal development of this idea than Westin, and the examples which he gives often make it difficult to be certain what he considers the essential evils of the "assault" which he deplores. Sometimes he seems concerned that personal-data systems collect and use more data than is really necessary. For example, at one point he writes,

> Every governmental agency, commercial enterprise, and academic discipline to which I have ever broached this subject fiercely insists that it cannot survive, let alone flourish, unless it has unbridled access to information and unregulated freedom to use data as it sees fit. . . . But I have a strong feeling that many of our data addicts could survive on considerably less than our informationally affluent society has to offer.[3]

Elsewhere, however, he seems most concerned about personal data filed without extenuating or explanatory information—in other words, about the dangers of not keeping *enough* data.[4]

Still other passages in *The Assault on Privacy* seem to suggest that modern methods of personal-data management are noxious in themselves. For example,

> In various medical centers, doctors are using computers to monitor physiological changes in the bodies of heart patients in the hope of isolating those alternations in body chemistry that precede a heart attack. The quest, of course, is to provide an "early warning system" so that treatment is not delayed until the actual heart attack, which often remedies the patient moribund for all practical purposes. But on the other side of the ledger, the same electronic sensors that can warn us of an im-

[2] See Ibid., pp. 25–26.
[3] Ibid., pp. 249–50.
[4] See Ibid., p. 33.

> pending heart attack can be used to locate us, track our movements, and measure our emotions and thoughts.[5]

This suggests that very powerful systems such as the one described here are too loaded with repressive potential to be trusted. Miller seems to argue the same point in passages like the following:

> It is axiomatic that the power the government can acquire through widespread surveillance or information control might be used to constrict individual freedom and that pressures in that direction must be resisted. Arguments or supplications couched in terms of governmental economy or administrative efficiency cannot justify every bureaucratic demand for greater power to extract, manipulate, store, and disseminate personal data. In the past these very objectives have been advanced, and fortunately rejected, as justifications for universal fingerprinting or passports for travel within the country.[6]

From such passages, of which *Assault on Privacy* offers a number, one could conclude that Miller favors outright blocking of the development of new surveillance systems, at least insofar as they could come to threaten personal freedom.

But other passages demonstrate Miller's faith in the apparently unlimited susceptibility of personal-data management to enlightened reform. For example,

> I am one who believes that although the new information technology has enormous long-range beneficial consequences for society, we must be concerned about the axiom—so frequently verified since the industrial revolution—that man must shape his tools lest they shape him.[7]

Elsewhere he uses the familiar language of "striking the balance" between privacy and its opposite; for example,

> To avoid any confusion on the point, it should be made clear that I do not oppose the development and uti-

[5] Ibid., p. 4.
[6] Ibid., p. 205.
[7] Ibid., pp. 7–8.

> lization of the information technologies and I do recognize that to gain the advantages offered by the computer we will have to strike new balances that may affect individual privacy.[8]

The contradictory impressions conveyed in passages like these demonstrate the imprecision of Miller's argument. These difficulties have much in common with Westin's failure to pursue the logical implications of his "balancing" argument. The deficiencies, however, are more serious in Miller's case. Miller never explains the nature of the evil he wishes to combat. Sometimes that evil seems to be the powers inherent in large surveillance systems. Sometimes it is inefficient or inaccurate use of data systems. Sometimes it is unauthorized data exchanges or other forms of unregulated bureaucratic cooperation. Nor is his notion of "balancing" very clearly developed. Sometimes the notion seems to require refraining from development of certain surveillance capabilities at all. More often it seems to demand only procedural guarantees like those envisaged by Westin; indeed, it is such suggestions which occupy much of the latter part of Miller's book. But then, in the last passage quoted above, by introducing the notion of "balancing" Miller suggests that losses to personal privacy may be necessary and inevitable.

Perhaps the failure of Miller and Westin to develop the central argument more rigorously is a result of having too many easy targets. They wrote these books at a time when public feeling about the privacy issue had just begun to coalesce. They sensed the existence of all sorts of "abuses" that people would find abhorrent, and they set out to give voice to this public outrage. Thus Miller's book abounds with reports of such things as a data bank on the children of migrant workers whose files were open to virtually anyone who asked, or of sloppy reporting practices among insurance-investigation firms which regularly led to insurance decisions based on inaccurate data.[9] Throughout his book, Miller offers example after scathing example of such abuses.

These books were among the first systematic attempts to bring these practices under public scrutiny. But the notorious

[8] Ibid., p. 8.
[9] Ibid., pp. 5, 69.

"abuses" which Miller and Westin single out are actually things hardly anyone would wish to defend. Such uses of personal data, in their effects, are both repugnant to individuals and ineffective from the standpoint of organizations.

The difficult questions arise where collection and use of personal data are both unpleasant or intrusive in themselves *and* essential to the attainment of some desired goal. Or when personal-data practices serve useful and important purposes *and* threaten to accrue overwhelming social power in the hands of those who maintain them. Miller does not provide much help here.

Miller and Westin seem to regard procedural reform as an absolute answer to the drawbacks posed by encroaching personal-data systems. Miller's concluding chapter discusses in turn "Technical Methods of Protection . . . ," "Procedural Methods of Improving Security," "Controls on Input, Output and Storage," and "Managing the Information Managers."[10] The section on technical measures recommends such things as electronic codes for access to computer files and scrambling of computer signals when these are carried through lines vulnerable to tapping. The following section suggests such expedients as the maintenance of a log of computer usage, and the designation of someone as what Miller calls "privacy ombudsman," "to ensure that the system was operating in the safest mode possible and to hear any disputes or complaints involving its practices."[11] The third series of recommendations propose restriction of personal data actually used to a bureaucratically necessary minimum, e.g., "computer programming techniques ought to be employed to prevent the output of data that are incomplete or have not been brought up to date."[12] The final section, "Managing the Information Managers," urges adoption of a forceful code of ethics by computer professionals. For anyone attentive to discussions of privacy protection in the use of computerized data files, such proposals will have a familiar ring. It is a measure of Miller's influence that his conclusions have had such a fundamental role in shaping discussion of these issues. But it is difficult to share his optimism.

[10] Ibid., pp. 239–57.
[11] Ibid., p. 248.
[12] Ibid., p. 250.

9 □ The Fair Credit Reporting Act (1970)

Privacy and Freedom and *The Assault on Privacy* were the most influential of many writings emanating from an increased awareness of the privacy problem. This awareness soon resulted in numerous legislative and policy changes. The first of these during this period—excluding the blockage of the National Data Center idea—was the Fair Credit Reporting Act. This act represented the first manifestation of a coherent official approach to regulation of personal-data systems. The consistency between the approach of this act and the principles enunciated in the recommendations of Westin and Miller bears special attention.

Before the 1970 legislation, credit reporting existed in a kind of legal and cultural limbo. Most people apparently did not know of the existence and activities of credit bureaus, except for a vague awareness of the importance of their "credit rating." Since credit bureaus never dealt directly with the people whose files they kept, the industry was largely invisible to the public. Indeed, there is a good deal of informal evidence that the credit-bureau industry and credit grantors sought to keep credit reporting out of the public eye—no doubt on the assumption that public understanding and concern could only complicate matters for them.[1] Moreover,

[1] Such, at any rate, was Rule's consistent impression in interviewing figures in the credit-reporting industry during the late 1960s, before federal legislation drew these activities forcefully to public notice.

credit bureaus were not ordinarily legally responsible for the content of their reports. Few people noticed the sweeping releases which they were required to sign on credit applications. These authorized the credit grantor to make virtually whatever investigations of the applicant he or she saw fit; the most usual of these was recourse to the credit agency.

Once these facts came to public attention, hardly anyone outside the credit industry had a word to say in defense of these practices. Nearly everyone felt that people ought to have some say in the handling of their information as it entered into credit decisions. The impact of the message was enhanced by numerous horror stories carried in newspapers and other periodicals. These related how faulty, negligent, incomplete reporting practices had poisoned people's credit files, and the files in turn had poisoned the people's lives through curtailment of credit or other privileges. Yet the victims in these unhappy events often did not know what had caused the damage; if they did understand the role of the credit bureau in their troubles, they could often seek redress only at the discretion of bureau personnel. Thus, by the late 1960s there seemed little question that some legislative action would be sought to change the picture. The only question was what principles such laws should embody.

The intent of the Fair Credit Reporting Act was, first, to create mechanisms for the public to understand credit-reporting practices and monitor the effects of these practices on their lives. Second, it was to establish ways of resolving differences over credit information between consumers, on the one hand, and credit bureaus and the buyers of their reports, on the other. Third, it was to create legal responsibilities on the part of bureaus to maintain certain minimum standards of care and competence in their reporting practices.

Often confused with credit reporting *per se* is the preparation of "investigative reports" on applicants for employment or insurance. Many consumer-credit bureaus also did some business, usually a rather small proportion of the total, in selling such reports. In preparing these reports, credit bureaus used roughly the same procedures followed by the insurance-reporting firms discussed in the preceding chapter. They sought to collect data not only on the subject's credit standing, but also on his or her community reputation, particularly with regard to drinking and other sensitive matters. Bureaus gathered data for these reports mainly through interviews with neighbors, acquaintances, and co-workers of the subject of the report. These activities came in for special criticism when credit reporting came under public scrutiny in the late 1960s. The Fair Credit Reporting Act attempts to make the same principles apply to both credit reporting in the strict sense and to these related practices.

The act specifies purposes for which bureaus may issue reports: screening of persons for credit, employment, insurance, and licensing and for use by any buyer who "otherwise has a legitimate business need for the information in connection with a business transaction involving the consumer." Another section of the act authorizes disclosure of "locator information"—names, addresses, and places of employment—to government agencies without subpoena. Police and other investigators routinely use such information. Thus the uses prescribed in the act include almost all the purposes for which organizations had traditionally used reports.

The act also sets time limits on reporting. Adverse data on such matters as previous credit accounts, unpaid tax liens, arrests, and suits or judgments must not be reported after seven years; bankruptcies can be noted for twice that long. These limitations are lifted, however, for reporting in connection with what were at the time considered especially large insurance and credit transactions and especially high-paying jobs. Because of inflation, however, this disclaimer now covers very large proportions of all credit accounts, insurance policies, and employment positions.

Other sections of the act require bureaus to disclose to consumers, at their request, "the nature and substance of all information" held in file—although the bureau is not actually required to show the inquirer his or her file or to provide a copy. This provision excludes medical information. Bureaus are required to disclose to the subjects of credit reports the sources of filed information, except for information compiled strictly for purposes of insurance or employment reporting. And consumers are entitled to access to the identities of all buyers of credit reports made on them within the previous six months.

The act requires reporting agencies to "make a reasonable effort to verify the identity of a new prospective user and the uses certified by such prospective user prior to furnishing" a report. "No consumer reporting agency may furnish a consumer report," the act continues, "if it has reasonable grounds for believing" that the report will be used for other than the authorized purposes. Bureaus are required to follow "reasonable procedures" to ensure "maximum possible accuracy" in their reporting. The act requires buyers of reports to refer customers to the reporting agency when reports result in adverse actions. It provides for civil damages to consumers where bureaus willfully and maliciously fail to comply with the act's provisions, and fines of up to $5,000 for those who give or obtain credit reports for other than authorized uses.

Finally, the Fair Credit Reporting Act makes provision for consumers to dispute the accuracy or completeness of data held in file. It calls on the bureau to reinvestigate such data "unless it has reasonable grounds to believe that the dispute by the consumer is frivolous or irrelevant." Should a dispute remain unresolved, the consumer may add a brief statement to the file, to be forwarded to future buyers of a report. Here again, however, the agency need not forward such a statement if it has "reasonable grounds to believe that it is frivolous or irrelevant."

Clearly the act does provide certain significant openings for consumers to exert an influence on the collection and use of information referring to them. The ability to check and dispute the content and uses of data has undoubtedly helped restrict the effects of inaccurate credit reporting. The potential legal sanctions against credit-bureau staff who fail to exercise "reasonable procedures" has undoubtedly cut down on misuses of credit information. The years since 1970 have thus almost certainly seen a rise in the efficiency, accuracy, and openness of credit reporting.[2]

Beyond these procedural improvements, what effect has the act had on the role of credit reporting in American life? Clearly one very important effect has been to legitimize these activities. Having operated, with increasing nervousness over the years, in a kind of legal vacuum, the credit-reporting industry now has official sanction and legal ground rules for its

[2] In our own survey of 291 Long Island residents, conducted in 1976–77, we found that of 103 respondents who reported having experienced problems with loan or credit transactions, 19 (18 percent) had examined their own credit records.

operations. The opening portions of the act include the following statements:

> The banking system is dependent upon fair and accurate credit reporting. Inaccurate credit reports directly impair the efficiency of the banking system, and unfair credit reporting methods undermine the public confidence which is essential to the continued functioning of the banking system. . . .
>
> Consumer reporting agencies have assumed a vital role in assembling and evaluating consumer credit and other information on consumers. . . .
>
> It is the purpose of this title to require that consumer reporting agencies adopt reasonable procedures for meeting the needs of commerce for consumer credit, personnel, insurance, and other information. . . .

None of the provisions of this legislation strikes seriously at any major established interest in the credit-reporting field. The interests of the general public are identified with the improved working of the systems. The goal is public acceptance of the system through greater public participation in its workings, rather than interference with any key element of information flow in consumer-credit reporting. At the price of a few quite moderate reforms, the credit-reporting industry obtained something close to official endorsement of its activities.

Arthur Miller, writing shortly after passage of the act, speaks critically of the politics involved:

> The original Proxmire bill had been butchered . . . Industry lobbyists and bank-oriented senators engaged in the dissection, while advocates of consumer protection quietly relied on the legislative process to produce a bill that would respond to the needs of the public.[3]

Miller goes on to criticize the act in detail for its failure to limit the purposes for which credit files could be examined, for its weak protections for the accuracy of credit-file data,

[3] Arthur R. Miller, *Assault on Privacy* (Ann Arbor, Mich.: University of Michigan Press, 1971), p. 86.

and for the cumbersome procedures which it requires for people to identify and rectify errors in their files.[4]

We can attest at first hand as to the industry role in shaping the bill. A staff member of the Associated Credit Bureaus, Inc., the national trade association, told James Rule not long after passage, "A lot of that bill was written right here [in ACB headquarters in Houston.]"[5] But we would note that Miller's objections are ones of degree, ones which still leave him within an emerging consensus concerning the regulation of personal-data systems. Miller believes that the bill should have gone further to make it easy for people to inquire about and to contest their credit records. But Miller endorses the key assumption underlying the act, i.e., that efficient transmission of the fullest and most accurate data for use in credit decision-making is inherently desirable. Thus he writes, in a slightly different context,

> Despite the concern I have expressed about a computerized consumer reporting industry, the desirability of employing the new technology cannot be doubted. Although concentration of power and reduced competition within the credit, computer, and communications industries pose threats, reasonable risks must be taken if we are to achieve a streamlined commercial exchange system.[6]

Miller's remarks here apply specifically to the centralization and monopolization involved in development of new, computerized consumer-credit systems. But his words clearly point to efficiency as the key criterion for the acceptability of credit reporting.

The belief that the systems are acceptable if they are efficient lies at the heart of the official response to the privacy issue. It is assumed that all parties to the credit transaction—consumer, bureau, and buyer of the report—share an interest in the efficiency of reporting. This leads to the

[4] Ibid., p. 87.

[5] Similarly, interviews by the present authors under way at the time of this writing have garnered a number of statements by credit-bureau officials affirming satisfaction with the effects of the Fair Credit Reporting Act.

[6] Miller, *Assault on Privacy,* p. 89.

conclusion that the greater the amount of information, the more accurate the information; and that the finer the decision-making, the better for all concerned. At first thought, all this may seem unexceptionable; yet other possibilities might well have been considered. Someone might have proposed an act which actually made *significant* restrictions on the forms of information which could be reported or on the length of time in which data could be held in file. Such measures might serve to prevent consumers who make "mistakes" in their use of credit from being penalized too much, or simply prevent the amassing of too much potentially abusable information in centralized stores. The following chapter considers some of these possibilities at greater length.

But the act doesn't do any of this. It forbids none of the traditional uses of credit reporting; it restricts the reporting of data only after the information would be obsolete anyway, and it makes no significant restrictions on bureaus' access to any form of data which they traditionally use. Moreover, the consumer access to credit information required by the act helps to ensure accuracy and completeness in the bureaus' "products." The net effect is to encourage efficiency within the industry and public acceptance of its practices, while leaving the interests of the credit industry in collecting and selling personal data untouched. Clearly this approach to "privacy protection" is vastly advantageous to established interests—much more than one which might call into question the ever-growing thoroughness and sophistication of credit surveillance.

10 □ Records, Computers and the Rights of Citizens (1973)

The July 1973 publication of the Report to the Secretary of the Department of Health, Education and Welfare by its Advisory Committee on Automated Personal Data Systems confirms the trend toward protection of vested interests in surveillance. The committee, composed of twenty-five members from government and private institutions, was chaired successively by Frances Grommers of the Harvard School of Public Health and by Willis Ware of the RAND Corporation; its members included Arthur R. Miller, author of *The Assault on Privacy*. The committee was created, according to the report, as "a cross-section of experienced and concerned citizens appointed by the Secretary . . . to analyze the consequences of using computers to keep records about people."[1] This body met intermittently between February 1972 and March 1973, with its day-to-day workings handled by a salaried staff. The actual drafting and editing of the final report were most likely the responsibility of the staff director,

[1] U.S. Department of Health, Education and Welfare, Secretary's Advisory Committee on Automated Personal Data Systems, *Records, Computers and the Rights of Citizens* (Washington, D.C.: U.S. Government Printing Office, 1973), p. xix.

David B. H. Martin, and of Carole W. Parsons, associate executive director.

The report, although neither a work of scholarship nor an act of law, clearly shows both the influences of Westin and Miller and marked similarities to the Fair Credit Reporting Act of 1970. At the same time, it embodied new elements, some of them of special interest here. Most important, the detailed recommendations embodied in the report have become the basis for further legislation. The report itself has received considerable attention and has been reissued as a commercial paperback, after considerable circulation in its original form as a government publication.[2] The report follows the same line of reasoning as Miller and Westin; erosion of personal privacy is attributed to technology as an intrusive force, upsetting existing social balances.[3] This force creates the risk of "abuse" of personal-information systems, abuse which demands corrective action.

Early in their discussion, the HEW writers imply that the drawbacks of modern personal-data systems are inherent in their structure. In discussing a proposed new system for storing patients' medical data and disseminating it to health-care staff, they write,

> The system is an elegant tool for addressing a complex set of social problems. It would be hard to argue that the patient population being cared for would be better off without the services the system makes possible. It is also apparent that knowing who an individual is, and the details of his medical history, can be of vital importance in treating patients, but the system has certain social control capabilities that should be noted nonetheless.
>
> . . . In discussing a system serving such patently humane purposes, words like "control" and "coercion" may have an objectionable ring, but the coercive *potential* of the surveillance component, especially in some other area of application, is evident.[4]

[2] U.S. Department of Health, Education and Welfare, *Records, Computers and the Rights of Citizens* (Cambridge, Mass.: MIT Press, 1973).
[3] Ibid., pp. 12–30.
[4] Ibid., pp. 25–26.

Passages like these lead one to expect the writers to counsel restraint in the creation of such systems, especially those whose potential for coercive use is especially striking. But such is not the case:

> We were not charged with developing criteria for determining when and for what purposes to establish personal data systems. It is doubtful that any such criteria are feasible or warranted.[5]

The bulk of the report, in fact, is devoted to recommendations based on the acceptance of such systems as a *fait accompli.*

The HEW writers describe three categories of personal information systems—administrative records, such as those used in consumer credit or Social Security; intelligence records, such as those maintained by law-enforcement or espionage organizations; and statistical records, such as those generated by sample surveys.[6] They adopt this division from Westin, and they add, "it is apparent that, by and large, administrative records are considered public; intelligence records, secret; and statistical records, anonymous."[7] They then treat intelligence records as not subject to the same demands of openness as other personal data. This, of course, effectively evades what would have been a major political issue.

The evils of administrative and statistical personal-record systems, for the HEW authors, are much the same as those attacked by Westin and Miller, and by the Fair Credit Reporting Act. They are failures of systems to achieve the purposes for which they were created, or failures to provide for awareness and participation of the subject of the records. As a basis for the reforms which they advocate, they cite five principles of "fair information practice." These have been so widely influential that they are worth quoting in detail:

> There must be no personal-data record-keeping systems whose very existence is secret.
>
> There must be a way for an individual to find out

[5] Ibid., p. 51.
[6] Ibid., pp. 5–6.
[7] Ibid., p. 6.

what information about him is in a record and how it is used.

> There must be a way for an individual to prevent information about him obtained for one purpose from being used or made available for other purposes without his consent.
>
> There must be a way for an individual to correct or amend a record of identifiable information about him.
>
> Any organization creating, maintaining, using, or disseminating records of identifiable personal data must assure the reliability of the data for their intended use and must take reasonable precautions to prevent misuse of the data.

Enunciating the overall philosophy guiding their recommendations, the HEW writers note,

> A record containing information about an individual in identifiable form must therefore be governed by procedures that afford the individual a right to participate in deciding what the content of the record will be, and what disclosure and use will be made of the identifiable information in it. Any recording, disclosure, and use of identifiable personal information not governed by such procedures must be proscribed as an unfair information practice unless such recording, disclosure or use is specifically authorized by law.

Then they continue,

> This formulation does not provide the basis for determining *a priori* which data should or may be recorded and used, or why, and when. It does, however, provide a basis for establishing procedures that assure that individual a right to participate in a meaningful way in decisions about what goes into records about him and how that information shall be used.[8]

The latter statement might stand as a motto for the entire

[8] Ibid., p. 41.

program of official reform of personal-data systems. Taking the existence and continued growth of surveillance for granted, these efforts concentrate on making the workings of these systems as efficient and as popularly acceptable as possible. The HEW writers seek to subject these systems to every form of reasoned evaluation—except that of whether their existence and growth are good things in the first place. The HEW authors do acknowledge that scrutiny of some systems may cast doubt on their necessity.[9] But they provide no suggestions for systematically analyzing the drawbacks of these systems; as a result, they implicitly concede that systems of personal-information use which are effective to their organizational ends must be considered acceptable.

As so often happens in official planning, the most important issues are decided by default in the HEW report. The most profound social choice at stake here is whether organizations will or will not develop more and more sophisticated uses for personal-data systems. Reasonable alternatives do exist for many, perhaps most, forms of bureaucratic surveillance. If the notion of "balancing" makes any sense at all, it is in considering the costs of such measures in relation to the gains they promise for the preservation of privacy. Yet the HEW report, like the other elements of the official response to these issues, fails even to recognize these important choices.

If the recommendations stemming from this principle were the only ones offered by the HEW group, their report might well represent the perfect expression of the narrow pursuit of bureaucratic efficiency. But there is a significant exception concerning the use of the Social Security number. Both government and private organizations, they note, find the Social Security number useful as a file number for all sorts of personal-data systems—whether or not the systems have anything to do with Social Security. Despite such usefulness, or indeed because of it, the HEW writers find the extension of its use disturbing. They ultimately recommend "against the adoption of any nationwide, standard, personal identification format, with or without the SSN, that would enhance the likelihood of arbitrary or uncontrolled linkage of records about people, particularly between government or govern-

[9] Ibid., p. 51.

ment-supported automated personal data systems."[10] Elsewhere, they recommend strict limitation of points where providing the number is legally required, and suggest that no one be asked to provide his or her SSN without being informed of the legal force of the request.[11]

Here the HEW authors have risen above their stated determination to avoid judging "which data may be recorded and used." We feel that the principles underlying such skepticism must receive much wider consideration if there is to be any more satisfactory response to the privacy issue.

[10] Ibid., p. 122.
[11] Ibid., pp. xxxii–xxxv.

11 □ The Privacy Act of 1974

The HEW report was published in July of 1973. No doubt it would have attracted attention under any circumstances, but the Watergate scandal enhanced that attention enormously. These were times when no one wanted to appear friendly to government surveillance over private persons. The Privacy Act of 1974 was written to apply the principles of the HEW report to the federal government's use of personal data. This legislation, it was hoped, would be a model for further legislation applying to private organizations.

The Privacy Act of 1974 follows the HEW recommendations quite closely. Like the recommendations, the Privacy Act steers clear of confrontation with most coercive or investigative record-keeping activities. The CIA and most law-enforcement record systems receive exemption from most of its provisions. Also exempt from some important provisions are record systems kept in connection with protection services for the President, certain background checks in connection with military and civilian federal employment, and a few other uses. Still, even with these exemptions, most federal personal record-keeping is subject to the provisions of the act.

With some exceptions, the Privacy Act limits disclosure from personal-data files to employees of the agency keeping the record who "have a need for the record in the performance of their duties"; to personnel of other agencies in connection with "routine uses" of the record for purposes "compatible with the purposes for which it was collected"; and to law-enforcement agencies. The phrasing obviously leaves much room for interpretation—even the definition of an agency or a record system can be problematic. There have been charges that some official definitions of "personal record system" have lumped more than one data system under a single declaration.[1]

Agencies are required to maintain only those records that are "relevant and necessary to accomplish" their missions. They are to collect personal information "to the greatest extent practicable from the subject individual," and to inform persons of the nature of the authority on which information is demanded of them. The act requires agencies to maintain all personal records with "such accuracy, relevance, timeliness, and completeness as is reasonably necessary to assure fairness to the individual." Clearly these provisions, too, admit of more than one interpretation.

Like the Fair Credit Reporting Act, the Privacy Act seeks to ensure access to one's own file and to allow a person to dispute its contents and request changes. If the record-keeping agency refuses to make changes, the individual may enter a supplementary statement of his or her own. As with credit files, these statements must be circulated to all users of the file.

The Privacy Act requires agencies to publish annual notice of "the existence and character" of each record system. This notification must include information on the coverage and effects of the system, and identify by title and business address the main agency official responsible. The agency must maintain a register of all but routine uses of the file, including the "date, nature and purpose of each disclosure to any person or to another agency." With some exceptions, these disclosures must be made available on request to the subject of the file. The act requires data-keeping agencies to take certain technical and managerial steps to safeguard the "security and confidentiality" of their files. The act provides for both civil remedies and criminal penalties in the event of violation, although these seem rarely to have been invoked.

[1] Privacy Protection Study Commission, *Personal Privacy in an Information Society* (Washington, D.C.: U.S. Government Printing Office, 1977), pp. 506–07.

Clearly, the "efficiency criterion" is still at work, with no critical evaluation of the need for personal-data systems in the first place. The approach is to construe "privacy protection" as ensuring that personal-data systems function as fairly, openly, and efficiently as possible. Such an approach creates a rich agenda for the absorption of would-be critics' energy in determining whether particular practices do, in fact, meet these standards. And in the ensuing controversies over these questions, key social choices are obscured.

12 □ The Report of the Privacy Protection Study Commission (1977)

The Privacy Act of 1974 also created the Privacy Protection Study Commission to conduct a "study of the data banks, automated data processing programs, and information systems of governmental, regional, and private organizations" and to recommend "the extent, if any" to which the provisions of the Privacy Act should be applied to them. This authorized the commission to study, and recommend changes in, virtually any major personal-data system. The commission had, ultimately, more than two years and $1,850,000 with which to pursue its efforts. The chairman was David Linowes, managing partner in a large New York accounting firm; the vice-chairman was Willis Ware of the RAND Corporation, who had served as chairman of the HEW committee. Other members of the commission were two Congressmen, one state senator, the president of a major insurance company, and the retired editor of a major daily newspaper. In addition, the commission relied on a relatively large and well-qualified professional staff. The executive director was Carole W. Parsons, formerly associate executive director of the HEW committee.

The key result of the commission's labors, the publication of *Personal Privacy in an Information Society,* came in July of 1977. In addition to 162 detailed recommendations, the

600-odd-page report and its five appendices include lengthy chapters on personal-data handling in consumer credit, banking, mailing lists, insurance, employment, medical care, and a number of other areas. It constitutes one of the most far-reaching inquiries into organizational uses of personal data ever assembled.

Though most of the report is devoted to studies of record-keeping practices in specific institutions, the long introductory chapter sets down the assumptions underlying the commission's thinking. As in other writings, the present status of the privacy issue is considered a result of technological "intrusions" into previously "balanced" social relationships. The Privacy Commission writers, however, take a more sophisticated view of these transformations, noting that they entail not only technological changes but also fundamental changes in our social relationships. For example, they stress the importance of discriminating decision-making as a force shaping personal data management:

> Organizations increasingly desire information that will facilitate fine-grained decisions about individuals. A credit-card issuer wants to avoid people who do not pay their bills, but it also strives to identify slow payers and well intentioned people who could easily get into debt beyond their ability to repay. Insurance companies seek to avoid people whose reputation or life style suggests that they may have more than the average number of accidents or other types of losses. Employers look for job applicants who give promise of being healthy, productive members of a work force.[1]

A number of these early observations on the sociology of the issue have much in common with the views on surveillance put forward in Part I. But most of the commission's recommendations aim at reform of these practices, reform based on the same efficiency considerations discussed earlier in this chapter. Early in the report, for example, the commission writers state the need to

[1] Privacy Protection Study Commission, *Personal Privacy in an Information Society* (Washington, D.C.: U.S. Government Printing Office, 1977), p. 5.

> strike a proper balance between the individual's personal privacy interests and society's information needs. In this report, the Privacy Protection Study Commission identifies the steps necessary to strike that balance. . . .[2]

As in the other elements of the official response to the privacy issue, this means creating a say for the individual in the treatment of his or her own records. Except for this, the report generally leaves unquestioned the growing powers of bureaucratic surveillance over individuals' lives.

The commission writers characterize the broader goals underlying their recommendations as follows:

> to create a proper balance between what an individual is expected to divulge to a record-keeping organization and what he seeks in return *(to minimize intrusiveness)*;
>
> to open up record-keeping operations in ways that will minimize the extent to which recorded information about an individual is itself a source of unfairness in any decision about him made on the basis of it *(to maximize fairness)*; and
>
> to create and define obligations with respect to the uses and disclosures that will be made of recorded information about an individual *(to create legitimate, enforceable expectations of confidentiality)*[3].

The detailed policy recommendations offered by the commission are in fact linked fairly closely to these three principles.

The fact that the recommendations offered by the Privacy Commission come to a total of 162 reflects the variety of institutions addressed, more than a multiplicity of underlying principles. Twenty-two Privacy Commission recommendations, for example, seek to ensure individuals' access to their own data files. Yet these recommendations entail the application of a handful of principles to record-keeping in insurance, employment, credit, and a number of other settings. The same pattern prevails in other areas where the Commission reiter-

[2] Ibid., p. 3.
[3] Ibid., pp. 14–15.

ates a given idea in slightly different form in recommendations applying to different kinds of record-keeping.

Other Privacy Commission recommendations aim at establishing accuracy, completeness, and timeliness in personal-data files. One recommendation, for example, requires that firms which mistakenly identify someone's check as bad in a report to a check-guarantee service be required to forward corrections when the error is detected. Another recommendation would require insurance organizations and the agencies which sell investigative reports on insurance applicants to maintain accuracy in their data. Again, similar recommendations apply to most of the other institutional forms of record-keeping covered in the report.

Other major categories of recommendations seek to circumscribe forms of information collected and means of collection. Still others aim to ensure the right to dispute and correct the contents of one's file, and to restrict the uses of personal information for particular decision-making purposes. The largest category of recommendations seeks to regulate disclosure from data files.

Some of the ideas behind the Privacy Commission's recommendations are new. The Fair Credit Reporting Act, the recommendations of the HEW committee, and the provisions of the Privacy Act all take established patterns in the collection of data by organizations more or less for granted. Certain recommendations of the Privacy Commission, by contrast, would limit collection of information. For example, the commission authors recommend against employers' recourse to arrest records on employees or applicants for employment.[4] Exceptions are envisaged where such checks are required by law, and the proscription does not apply to records of conviction. The commission also recommends against the use of the polygraph by employers.[5] It recommends that credit grantors notify applicants of the nature and sources of information to be sought about them.[6] Another

[4] Ibid., p. 243. It should be noted that this recommendation, like most other commission recommendations relating to employment, is a recommendation for voluntary action on the part of employers, rather than for legislation. Nor does this recommendation apply to the investigations of reporting firms.

[5] Ibid., pp. 239–40.

[6] Ibid., p. 76.

recommendation enjoins employers from seeking information on applicants other than that "relevant to specific decisions."[7]

The Privacy Commission writers try to limit disclosure of personal data much more than before. The HEW recommendations, and the provisions of the Privacy Act which follow from them, limit disclosure to "purposes compatible" with the original provision of information. The Privacy Commission recommendations are more specific. One recommendation opposes disclosure from public-assistance files without the recipient's permission, except as otherwise stipulated by statute.[8] Elsewhere, the commission recommends tightening protections against federal investigatory access to bank-account information without the individual's permission. Under this recommendation, individuals would have the right to challenge subpoenas or administrative summons of their bank records or other personal papers held by institutions.[9] The Privacy Commission writers attach considerable importance to these more aggressive departures from immediate precedent, regarding them as reflecting their special concern for minimizing intrusiveness and protecting confidentiality.

Certain of these recommendations indeed do represent new departures. In some cases they even turn away from exclusive concern with efficiency as a guide for the protection of privacy. Restricting the use of arrest records, for example, denies employers a form of information which might actually, from their point of view, provide an advantage in screening applicants. A number of other restrictions on what would be bureaucratically efficient uses of personal data are to be found throughout the commission's recommendations. In general, though, the Privacy Commission recommendations follow the pattern familiar in earlier efforts: enhancement of efficiency in organizational use of personal data, in conjunction with individual participation in these practices.

There are only modest exceptions to these generalizations. Only a few of their recommendations, for example, would deny organizations useful information. Limitation of government access to "private papers" (bank records and other

[7] Ibid., p. 237.
[8] Ibid., pp. 476–77.
[9] Ibid., pp. 362–65.

personal files held by private institutions) is one; the recommended curtailment of polygraph use by employers is another. There are a few other clear-cut examples. But most of the recommendations on collection and disclosure of personal data amount to demands for efficiency and openness in inherently unequal and privacy-invading practices. Thus one recommendation proposes that public-assistance and social-service agencies make inquiries aimed at establishing the eligibility of applicants "in a manner that, to the maximum extent possible, does not reveal the specific nature of the service sought by the client."[10] Or, in the treatment of tax information, the recommendation that disclosures of IRS data to the Parent Locator Service be limited "to the minimum necessary to locate an alleged absent parent."[11] If one accepts the wisdom and legitimacy of the practices in question, these recommendations make sense. They amount to good advice to the institutions concerned to keep their privacy-invading practices to the minimum necessary to attain their appointed ends.

But in most cases, the efforts to limit intrusion and assure confidentiality are unlikely to be effective in practice. The commission's recommendations suggest that credit and insurance institutions notify an individual, at the time of application, about the nature of the investigation to be made in considering the application. The writers offer this recommendation in the stated hope of making "market forces work to the advantage" of the applicant by enabling him to "take his business elsewhere," should the proposed investigation seem too intrusive.[12] But a major reduction in the intrusiveness of these inquiries through competition among credit and insurance firms is unlikely; the power position of the firms on other counts and the complexity, for the individual, of comparing these requirements militate against this. Likewise, recommendations which offer the individual formal say in disclosure of personal information would not necessarily lead to authentic choice in the matter. The commission recommends, for example, that individuals have the right to grant or withhold information from their own medical files.[13] The recommendation is hedged with a number of exceptions, but,

[10] Ibid., p. 464.
[11] Ibid., p. 553.
[12] Ibid., p. 193.
[13] Ibid., pp. 306–07.

even apart from this, it would not provide an effective barrier to access, say, by insurance companies. Most people need insurance, and would have to give whatever information insurance companies can legally require.

The seriousness of the commission's efforts are impressive, but not equal to the social forces which weigh against privacy. In its efforts to "minimize intrusiveness," the commission writers virtually accept the legitimacy of inherently intrusive practices. In its attempt to "protect confidentiality," they take as given processes where circulation of personal information inheres. Powerful political forces stand behind the increasing demands by organizations for personal data. With a few notable exceptions, the commission recommendations do not challenge those forces. For the most part, the 162 recommendations read like a manual for making surveillance as publicly acceptable as possible—consistent with its expansion and efficiency.

"We live, inescapably," the commission authors write, "in an 'information society,' and few of us have the option of avoiding relationships with record-keeping organizations."[14] Yet some things are more "inescapable" than others. The more than 600 pages of the Privacy Commission's report offer virtually no systematic discussion of possible alternatives to the drift into the "information society." They do not consider simply dispensing with the Parent Locator Service, as a method of surveillance and control not worth its price in intrusion. They do not take up the possibility of doing without the unseemly activities of insurance-investigative firms. They do not explore the potential for cutting back drastically the amount and kinds of information allowed to bear on credit decisions. They do not take seriously the possibility of seeking less discriminatory, less "information-intensive" alternatives to bureaucratic surveillance. Surely these alternatives deserve serious consideration in any thoughtful approach to the protection of privacy.

[14] Ibid., p. 5.

13 □ The Emergent Consensus

Before 1967, no such thing as "privacy policy" existed, either in the United States or abroad. By 1977, however, the Privacy Protection Study Commission could publish its recommendations as an enlargement and refinement of established policies. In the interim, the writings, reports, public controversies, and legislative efforts discussed above had shaped public understanding of the requirements of "privacy protection." The result was a consensus on general principles which policy-makers would apply to a wide variety of personal-data systems. These principles bear considerable, though largely unnoticed, political implications.

The laws and writings discussed above obviously do not exhaust the list of such efforts. Not only have other writings and legislation addressed the same issues at the federal level, other privacy legislation has been proposed and enacted in the states. And abroad, serious legislative activity has taken place in other parliamentary democracies among the developed nations.

Sweden, West Germany, and France, at the time of this writing, have enacted their own personal-data protection acts. These three bodies of legislation share with our own Privacy Act of 1974 and Fair Credit Reporting Act, and with the recommendations of the HEW committee and of the Privacy Protection Study Commission, a concern with five broad principles: establishing access to one's own data; ensuring accuracy, completeness, and timeliness of recorded information; limitation on information which may be collected; establishing procedures for challenging and correcting erroneous data; and protecting data from unnecessary disclosure. Each of the seven bodies of legislation and recommendations entail provisions aimed at implementing most of these five principles. Most other legislation proposed or enacted in the individual states in America or in foreign countries concentrates more narrowly on one or a few of the five principles.

The privacy issue took root in the United States before anywhere else, and the American influence abroad is marked. We have never encountered any foreign writings on the subject, for example, which did not rely heavily, in one way or another, on Alan Westin's work. But there are differences among countries, especially in the role envisaged for specialized privacy-protecting institutions. Privacy-protection measures envisaged or enacted in Canada, Britain, France, Sweden, Denmark, and West Germany have all entailed creation of some sort of governmental or semi-official board for supervision of personal-data systems. In most cases these bodies would be licensing authorities, something like the American Federal Communications Commission. They would have powers to inspect the data banks and represent the privacy interests of individuals *vis à vis* the data-keepers. American planning, at least at the federal level, has not taken this direction. Administration forces successfully opposed provisions of the Privacy Act of 1974 which would have created a permanent, powerful Privacy Board. The Privacy Protection Study Commission—a research and advisory body with a two-year life span—represented the vestige of that defeated proposal. The Privacy Commission did in turn recommend the creation of a federal "entity" to monitor privacy statutes and carry out research on matters related to privacy. However, its only enforcement authority, according to the Commission authors, should be "in connection with the implementation by federal agencies of the Privacy Act itself."[1] Rather than attempting to create a new institu-

[1] Privacy Protection Study Commission, *Personal Privacy in an Information Society* (Washington, D.C.: U.S. Government Printing Office, 1977), p. 37.

tion to give force to its own recommendations, the Privacy Commission attempts to enable individuals to protect their own privacy by creating specific procedures for them to enforce their demands against data-keeping organizations.

14 □ Selective Perceptions

By the time the Privacy Commission submitted its recommendations in 1977, the dominance of the efficiency criterion in privacy-protection policy and legislation was nearly complete. Yet the emergence of this approach had not been for want of other possibilities. Since the earliest debates in the 1960s, more fundamental and more effective approaches had been considered. The testimony from early Congressional hearings, for example, often envisaged sweeping efforts to curtail the growth of surveillance systems themselves. Sometimes these statements have come even from Representatives and Senators themselves. Recall the fate of the National Data Center—rebuffed by Congressional opposition, ostensibly because of privacy concerns. It may have been that the objections offered publicly here were not the true political reasons for this opposition. But the fact remains that public officials were willing to proclaim their opposition to development of personal-data systems on the grounds that such systems were dangerous or pernicious in themselves.

Among scholarly writers, skepticism about the social effects of technological change in general, as well as about surveillance in particular, have long been common.[1] A good exam-

[1] See Jacques Ellul, *The Technological Society* (New York: Alfred A. Knopf, 1964) and Joseph Weizenbaum, *Computer Power and Human Reason* (San Francisco: W. H. Freeman, 1976), especially chapter 10.

ple among the privacy debates of the last fifteen years is the testimony given by Paul Armer, the noted computer scientist, on the repressive potentials of computerized payment systems.[2] Statements by legal scholars Kent Greenawalt and Milton Wessell offer other examples of such skepticism.[3] Indeed, sometimes Westin and Miller imply that some surveillance systems are simply too sweeping to warrant the risks of developing them. But these two influential writers never draw from such statements what we would consider their logical implications for policy.

Further, even some official writings on privacy betray ambivalence about using powerful surveillance techniques, even under procedural safeguards. The HEW report, while officially foreswearing judgment on the wisdom of establishing particular data systems, did take a clear-cut stand against extension of Social Security numbering. Gestures like this run against the usual direction of privacy legislation and policy.

Some of the most sensitive observations on the limitations of the efficiency criterion, in fact, are to be found in the Report of the Privacy Protection Study Commission. An appendix of that report dealing with the effects of the 1974 Privacy Act notes that

> problems perceived by the Congress at the time of the . . . [1974 Privacy] Act's passage have turned out to be more complex than anticipated, and by and large they are independent of the problem of premeditated abuse. Actual or potential information abuses are much more likely to result from continuing growth in the government's appetite for information about individuals and in the use of that information for growing numbers and types of purposes. *The real danger is the gradual erosion of individual liberties through the automation, integration, and interconnection of many small, separate*

[2] See his testimony before the joint hearings of the Subcommittee on Constitutional Rights of the U.S. Senate Judiciary Committee and the Subcommittee on Science and Technology of the Senate Committee on Commerce, June 23, 1975.

[3] Kent Greenawalt, *Legal Protection of Privacy* (Washington, D.C.: Office of Telecommunication Policy, 1975); Milton R. Wessel, *Freedom's Edge: The Computer Threat to Society* (Reading, Mass.: Addison-Wesley, 1974).

record-keeping systems, each of which alone may seem innocuous, even benevolent, and wholly justifiable.[4]

One could not ask for a more precise criticism of the efficiency criterion. Reading carefully through the commission's report, one notes a number of equally telling statements to this same effect. And indeed a few of the commission's recommendations propose to sacrifice efficiency to what we would regard as more compelling values. But few of the officially sanctioned reform measures have threatened the existence of any major form of bureaucratic surveillance. The intent of reform measures has most often been to normalize the practices involved—minimizing the harm they cause to individuals while ratifying the desirability of the surveillance itself. Operating on such reformist assumptions, the privacy-protection movement thus gives the appearance of approving even the most dubious surveillance practices, such as inquiries by insurance firms into the moral repute of insurance applicants.

The remarkable thing is that the efficiency criterion makes such outcomes seem utterly natural. If one views the essential evils of personal-data systems as their failure to work efficiently—that is, to permit accurate, informed, timely decisions on the persons concerned—then it can be no more than natural to "reform" such systems by making them work more efficiently in these respects. It may well be that such reform may require collection of *more* personal data, in order to afford more exact, more just decision-making. The logic of the efficiency criterion for privacy protection would thus at least allow us to boast that we are preserving our privacy, even while yielding more and more of our data to organizations.

These bizarre implications of the official views dramatize the inadequacies of the underlying concepts. Indeed, official planning has systematically ignored the most important issue: the cumulative effects of widening bureaucratic surveillance upon social life as a whole. In the wholly worthwhile effort to protect people from injustice, inefficiency, or incompetence in

[4] Privacy Protection Study Commission, *Personal Privacy in an Information Society* (Washington, D.C.: U. S. Government Printing Office, 1977), Appendix 4, *The Privacy Act of 1974: An Assessment*, pp. 107–08.

the treatment of their data, planners have conveniently forgotten that the growth of bureaucratic surveillance may be unacceptable even when efficiency, due process, and openness of the systems are assured. The question ought to be, What price are we willing to pay for the continued extension of surveillance? In the long run, the answer to this question will surely be more important than the protection from procedural abuses which have preoccupied official planners thus far.

There are many reasons for seeking limits to the extension of bureaucratic surveillance—not simply as a source of unfairness or inefficiency, but as a bad thing in itself. The simplest of these reasons is what we have termed "aesthetic" reactions against intensive surveillance. No one really wants to live in a world where every previously private moment becomes a subject of bureaucratic scrutiny. There is something inherently desirable, at least for most people, about preserving private areas of experience.[5] Even where the ends of surveillance are impeccable, even where the agencies concerned carry out their monitoring with full rectitude and discretion, the monitoring of *every* moment would strike most people as unacceptable.

To be sure, present surveillance systems have hardly brought us to the point of total monitoring. But, as we argue in the following chapter, the logic of change in these systems suggests no "natural limit" to their extension. As long as efficiency criteria continue to guide the development of these systems, their attentions will continue to spread over larger and larger areas of what had been private experience.[6] The proper limit to this spread can only be identified through earnest debate and thoughtful reflection on the values of privacy and autonomy *versus* those of efficiency. We have no grounds for assuming that such debate and reflection would yield consensus. But this hardly justifies ignoring the incontestable fact that modern surveillance systems promise

[5] This seems to be the position of Charles Fried, in his article "Privacy," *Yale Law Journal*, Vol. 77, January 1968.

[6] This growth in the demands of modern surveillance systems may nevertheless be mitigated by the loosening of surveillance demands from more traditional bodies such as the family or neighborhood. See James B. Rule, *Private Lives and Public Surveillance* (New York: Schocken, 1974), especially pp. 331–33.

eventually to reach the limits of aesthetic acceptability by everyone's standards.

Another reason for limiting the unrestricted growth of bureaucratic surveillance lies in the value of preserving what one might term a desirable "looseness" in social relations. Other differences notwithstanding, many if not most surveillance systems work to make people responsible for their pasts. Criminal records ensure that people do not escape the repercussions of their criminal acts; insurance reporting works to link disreputable people to their community reputations; credit reporting helps credit grantors hold people responsible for their past credit-using behavior.

Most Americans probably feel that these processes are legitimate and desirable—at least in some measure. But most people probably also feel that there ought to be limits to the extent that people's "records" are held against them. Statements like the following from a spokesman for the country's largest insurance- and employment-reporting firm do leave one a little uneasy:

> It is a fact that the interchange of business information and the availability of record information imposes a discipline on the American citizen. He becomes more responsible for his performance whether as a driver of his car, as an employee in his job performance, or as a payor to his creditors. But this discipline is a necessary one if we are to enjoy the fruits of our economy and the present freedom of our private enterprise.[7]

Is a system of soliciting and reporting accounts of people's lives from friends, neighbors, and co-workers really essential to the enjoyment of "freedom"? More generally, is it desirable that people always be held fully responsible for all of what prospective employers, creditors, or insurers would consider their past shortcomings?[8] True, conventional wisdom in America endorses the notion that people must "reap as they sow." But popular sentiment also endorses the worth of "a

[7] From testimony before the House Committee on Government Operations, 90th Congress, 2nd Session, 16 May 1968, p. 5.

[8] This argument is developed ably by Kent Greenawalt in his *Legal Protections of Privacy,* p. 92.

fresh start" or "a clean slate." Systematic "forgetting" of people's pasts, even when troublesome from the standpoint of bureaucratic efficiency, may reflect a social value of considerable importance. Whether the values of efficiency or those of "wiping the slate clean" ought to prevail in any particular setting is bound to be a contentious issue. We do not insist on any particular resolution of the issue; indeed, the nature of the choices seems to us to preclude any programmatic "solution," apart from piecemeal compromises on a case-by-case basis. But we do insist that the issue must be confronted directly, and that the interests of efficiency alone cannot serve as a satisfactory basis for such confrontation. Again, the official response to the privacy issue has most often obscured these agonizing choices, precisely where they need to be dramatized.

A third compelling reason for limiting the growth of surveillance has to do with the potential of these systems for fostering excessive concentrations of power in society. Systems like those considered in this book—which collect pertinent data on literally millions of people and make such data available for law enforcement, taxation, credit, insurance, and related bureaucratic purposes—inevitably bring about change in relations between what Shils calls "centers" of social power and the "peripheries." For surveillance makes it possible for those at the centers to monitor the activities of large populations and "reach out" with forceful actions to shape and control those behaviors. Such capabilities may readily be used for oppressive purposes, regardless of the intentions which guided their creation in the first place. Income-tax systems may become vehicles for monitoring and persecuting political dissidents. Credit-card files and similar "private-sector" data systems may be appropriated by government for the same purpose, and to equal advantage. The results of increasing, through surveillance, the powers of institutions over individuals cannot necessarily be foreseen when surveillance systems are established.

These powers need not always be exercised in order to have their undesirable effects. We must recall the chilling effect which stems from pople's knowledge of the data-monitoring capabilities of centralized institutions.[9] The last ten

[9] See Wessel, *Freedom's Edge*, p. 30.

years have certainly altered many Americans' views of what centralized institutions, especially government ones, are capable of in these respects. Now it is much more difficult to dismiss the possibility of having one's phone tapped, one's tax returns used for political purposes, or one's life history recorded in a CIA file. The realization that these activities *might* take place, whether they really do or not in any particular instance, has potentially destructive effects on the openness of social systems to innovation and dissent. Clearly the best way to eliminate such threats is to limit surveillance.

We must remember that the purposes governing the use of surveillance systems can only be the purposes of those who control them at any particular point. A sophisticated system for monitoring people's health and administering prompt medical care could also be used to collect debts or to monitor and harass political dissidents. Whether such abhorrent possibilities become realities depends on the political and social climate in which surveillance operates, not on the original intent of those who found the system. Given that the development of repressive political intentions by those in power is always possible in some degree, some surveillance capabilities are simply too awesome to be worth developing. At some point, in other words, the repressive *potential* of even the most humane systems must make them unacceptable. Again, thoughtful and conscientious people will not find it easy to agree where a given system passes that point. Our concern here, however, is not to insist on our own judgments about any particular case, but rather to demand that people acknowledge the necessity of making such judgments.

In considering such questions, it must be remembered that meaningful protection of privacy extends considerably beyond one's narrow interest in avoiding misuse of one's own data. We suffer from excessive surveillance not only when it is used against us, but also when its real or threatened workings stifle freedom of action which others might enjoy. Just as with freedom of speech, all share an interest in the freedom of all from unjust, intimidating surveillance.

These observations, however, suggest reexamination of fundamental social directions. And political process in America does not easily assimilate such possibilities. The usual response is to carry out only those measures of reform which are comfortable to established interests. Thus the selection of those privacy concerns which appear most susceptible to reform within the context of existing social power relations; and thus the interpretation of "privacy protection" as the pursuit of these relatively narrow ends alone. This style of reform has a long pedigree in American political life. A brief look at its workings may show the selective perceptions which have shaped the privacy issue in a more familiar light.

15 □ Reform and the Domestication of Popular Discontent

The assimilation of the privacy issue has much in common with other events in American political and social history. Indeed, the "natural history" of domestication of contentious issues seems to represent one of the basic sequences of American public life.[1] The periodic high-water points of public dissatisfaction with the exercise of power by private forces have brought new forms of regulation and new agencies for enforcing institutional compliance with "the public interest." As a result, it is now impossible to watch television, have a prescription filled, take a train or a bus, or purchase a roast for dinner without partaking of at least one federally regulated activity. Recent proposed and enacted privacy legislation obviously will add a good many more entries to this list.

What larger significance can one attribute to this recourse to federal regulation? Should it be interpreted as evidence that all the special advantages of the previously unregulated interests have been extinguished? This, of course, has been a

[1] Readers familiar with the work of Theodore Lowi will note the deep affinities of the following discussion, and indeed of the interpretations offered throughout this book, to his approach. The basic reference is *The End of Liberalism* (New York: Norton, 1969).

perennial point of controversy among analysts of American politics. The optimistic interpretation, associated with centrist liberalism, has it that the imposition of regulation, either in the form of oversight institutions or of other safeguards, effectively guarantees the curtailment of the objectionable practices being regulated. The more skeptical interpretation, associated more with the political left, holds that imposition of regulatory measures has typically served to take the steam out of grass-roots protest, while leaving few, if any, meaningful checks on the regulated institutions.[2]

As evidence for the latter position, the critics can readily point to the flaccidity of bodies like the FCC and the highly mixed record, at best, of the federal government in pressing anti-trust actions. Or they might cite the extreme rarity in American history of anything resembling life-and-death conflicts between the central political powers and major private interests. Against these assertions, the centrists offer a simple rejoinder: If regulation really does not represent a significant constraint on the institutions subjected to it, how can one explain what appears as the spirited, indeed often bitter, opposition of these bodies to efforts to impose the regulation?[3] Surely the rough-and-tumble controversies which lead to regulation attest to the seriousness of the issues at stake. If, let us say, regulated industries really find federal regulation a convenient Trojan horse for the more efficient pursuit of their interests, as the critics charge, why do they go to such lengths to avoid regulation?

The answer to this question, at least in the case of the "privacy-protection" movement, is that the more hidebound representatives of the institutions under attack simply did not realize that a measure of regulation was the only thing which could save them from even more sweeping consequences. The shrewder representatives of survillance organizations were those who realized at the beginning that a blunted program of "reform" would actually consolidate their position. Certainly this pattern has many parallels in other forms of regulation. Alfred Chandler, not exactly known as a critic of

[2] See Theodore Lowi, *The Politics of Disorder* (New York: Basic Books, 1971), especially Chapter 1.
[3] See, for example, Talcott Parsons, *Structure and Process in Modern Societies* (Glencoe, Ill.: The Free Press, 1960), pp. 213–14.

business institutions, put it this way in referring to the New Deal's "reform" of Wall Street:[4]

> The only institution capable of stopping this economic descent was the federal government. During the 1930s, it began to undertake this role, but with great reluctance. . . . And managers and businessmen, those who had the most to gain, were among the most outspoken critics of the few moves that were made.

While it is harder to document the attitude of institutional elites toward the privacy-protection movement, it is clear that those who acceded to reform have acted shrewdly. Not only have most record-keeping organizations paid a modest price in curtailment of their freedom of action; they have also gained a fundamental advantage. That is an interpretation of "privacy protection" which legitimizes the extension and perfection of personal-data systems, so long as the systems can be shown to be efficient and relatively open in the decision-making they afford.[5]

In many respects, we agree that the efficiency of personal-data management benefits both organizations and data subjects. But to make this criterion the key consideration in judging the acceptability of such systems is a very serious mistake. The efficiency criterion may provide an endlessly comforting sleight-of-hand for ruling the most difficult questions out of order, and thus for avoiding considerations which might lead to fundamental criticisms of established institutions. But we hold that such avoidance, on careful examination, ultimately works to obscure the most significant historical choices.

[4] Alfred D. Chandler, Jr., *The Visible Hand: The Managerial Revolution in American Business* (Cambridge, Mass.: Belknap/Harvard University Press, 1977), p. 496.

[5] Our own recent interviews with officials of record-keeping organizations suggest that they are aware of the overall benefits which have accrued to their position through these controversies. One representative of an insurance reporting firm, commenting on the effects of the privacy issue in its prevailing interpretation, noted, "It has legitimized what we do . . . it has thrown light on the whole underwriting process and taken it out of the closet, so to speak." Commenting on the Fair Credit Reporting Act, he remarked, "It's permitted us to work in a litigation-free atmosphere with the consumer."

PART III

Prospects for the Future

The issues posed by personal-data systems would be thorny enough even if these practices were static. But of course this is not the case. Nearly every commentator has pictured present realities as transient manifestations of much deeper change. The demands of bureaucracies for personal data on all of us are greater than they have been in the past, but less than they are liable to be in the future. How are we to grasp the larger dimensions of these historic changes?

Consider this array of ordinary experiences: undergoing and paying for treatment at a hospital or clinic; registering at a hotel, and then paying the bill; taking part in a political demonstration; depositing a large sum in one's local bank account; receiving one's weekly or monthly pay; being stopped by a police officer on the highway; making a credit purchase; registering and insuring one's automobile; applying for welfare or some other social benefit. One could rate these and other ordinary experiences according to the following criteria: How many people, other than the parties to them, are aware that they occur; whether, and to what extent, the occurrence is recorded in documentary or other permanent form; how many people have access to such documentation; how long such data may be preserved; how frequent is the recourse to such information; and how important the real or potential consequences of such recourse may be to the original parties.

These ratings would largely capture the extent to which these encounters become subject to bureaucratic surveillance. *Surveillance represents a key source of characteristically modern demands on personal privacy.*

A fundamental trend of our times is the incorporation and use of more and more personal data from encounters like those listed above in processes of organizational surveillance. The local police officer may check the names of people he stops against computerized master lists of persons of interest to larger law-enforcement agencies, for example. Banks forward information on large transactions to government agencies. Similar observations could be made in all of these instances. All of these linkages of once relatively private experiences to larger processes of bureaucratic monitoring are relatively recent occurrences. Moreover, the development of modern, centralized social institutions leads to qualitatively new relationships—income taxation is an example—which involve people in new forms of surveillance. The demands of formal organizations for data on the persons with whom they deal mark the growing importance of such organizations in the life of modern, highly developed societies. Technological and social change conspire to make the data more intensively used and more sweeping in their effects.

These changes do entail certain compensations. The growth of centralized surveillance and control is accompanied by relaxation of privacy- and autonomy-eroding demands from neighbors, family, and kin. But in the longer run, we cannot ignore the distinctive dangers and disadvantages associated with the growth of bureaucratic (as distinct from informal) surveillance.

The secular rise in modern forms of surveillance and control clearly raises fundamental social and historical issues. How do these changes bear on key social values? What kind of social order is emerging from these trends? Perhaps most important, what end point is implicit in these patterns of change? Where are we heading, and do we really wish to make the trip? The official response to "the privacy issue" and the standard writings on the subjects scarcely address these questions.

16 □ Westin and Baker: Databanks in a Free Society (1972)

One of the few studies to touch on these issues at all is *Databanks in a Free Society*, by Alan Westin and Michael Baker.[1] This work examines the privacy implications of the change from manual to computerized systems of personal-data management in some fifty-five formal organizations, both public and private. Begun late in 1969 under the sponsorship of the National Academy of Sciences and the Russell Sage Foundation, this work capitalized on the acclaim which had surrounded *Privacy and Freedom*. In the years since its publication, *Databanks in a Free Society* has become nearly as fundamental a reference in the literature on this subject as the earlier work.

The concerns which led to the commissioning of the research were anxieties, especially widespread in the late 1960s, about the impact of the computer upon personal privacy. The authors characterize these concerns as follows:

> Many public commentators focused on technological possibilities, assuming that what could be done in a laboratory or in the environment of a special project would inevitably, and soon, become widespread organizational

[1] Alan F. Westin and Michael A. Baker, *Databanks in a Free Society* (New York: Quadrangle/New York Times Book Co., 1972).

> practice. Other commentators relied on the long-range system plans and project proposals of organizations, assuming that the goals and timetables portrayed there would be achieved as stated. With a sense of such rapidly accelerating change, legislators and judges began to wonder how they could intervene to bring this mushrooming technology under legal and administrative controls.[2]

Thus, the authors explain, the sponsors of the research sought to clarify the actual state of these changes and hence to facilitate enlightened policy.

The book begins with a short survey of computer technology, and a brief review, adapted from *Privacy and Freedom,* of legal developments in the privacy field. The bulk of the text is devoted to presentation and interpretation of data on fifty-five computerizing organizations. Nearly 200 pages are devoted to "profiles," or qualitative descriptions, of fourteen organizations considered leaders in computerized personal-record keeping. These discussions depict the current state of computer usage in these organizations, the changes that such use has brought about in management procedures, and the apparent trends in computerized record-keeping. The next section reports the results of the inquiries to all fifty-five organizations. These discussions deal with the conditions which led to computerization, comparisons of privacy aspects of computerized versus manual personal-data systems, and the effects of computerization on due process in information use. Another section of the book examines the implications of these findings for public policy. The book closes with three appendices: a survey of managerial opinion about the impact of computing on record-keeping, a presentation of recent public-opinion surveys on privacy issues, and a survey of databank developments in foreign countries.

The authors of *Databanks in a Free Society* clearly believe that the effects of computing on personal privacy have been exaggerated. Indeed, they devote much of the book to refuting the notion that computing moves organizations in directions different from those implied by preexisting organizational interests. Westin and Baker identify few if any

[2] Ibid., pp. 4–5.

instances where, during the period covered by their study, computing has occasioned the collection of new forms of personal data. Instead, they find that computing has much more often served to streamline the functioning of existing data systems and accommodate higher rates of activities in these systems. Nor has computing often seemed to bring about changes in the *kinds* of data stored by organizations. The authors report no clear direction of change in the state of personal privacy which can be attributed to computing. Rights of access to filed data, the freedom of exchange among data-keeping organizations, the quality of decision-making based on data files—all these things seem to vary in the same range after computerization as before. If one could identify any overall trend, it would be in the direction of greater organizational control over computerized than over manual files.

The strengths of *Databanks in a Free Society* lie in the ordering and presentation of very large amounts of material in clear and readable fashion. At least twenty researchers took part in gathering the data from the fifty-five organizations studied in the book, and the imposition of a coherent structure on these results represents an achievement in itself. It is easy to imagine the findings of such a far-reaching inquiry becoming lost in a sea of empirical detail.

But measured against the larger issues of the future of personal-data systems, the book shows serious shortcomings. In various ways, the shortcomings stem from the use of an analytical approach too superficial for the questions at hand. For a work written and largely researched by social scientists, *Databanks in a Free Society* is a remarkably journalistic book. Yet the intellectual tools of journalism do not suffice to deal with the issues which any study on these matters must confront.

Part of the difficulties lie with the relations between the methods of data-gathering used by the researchers and certain of their conclusions. The fifty-five computerizing organizations depicted in the inquiry were located in various cities in the East, the Midwest, and the West. These were both private and governmental bureaucracies engaged in a wide variety of activities involving personal-record keeping. The actual data-gathering in the Westin-Baker study took place mainly through site visits, or field interviews at organizational offices. According to the authors, these visits lasted between one and three days and involved between two and five interviewers. The authors report that an average of ten informants took part in each site visit.[3] Written material including newspaper accounts and documentation from the organization itself were reviewed to supplement the interviews, both before and after the visits. In most instances a single site visit apparently sufficed, but the authors note that "follow-up visits or extensive telephone conversations were made when necessary to complete our inquiries or update our files."[4]

Such an approach would certainly serve to enable the leadership of an organization to convey its own picture of its workings. But it would not meet accepted standards for field investigations where officials may knowingly or unknowingly provide misleading information. For example, in discussing the accuracy of newly computerized files, the authors write that the managers and employees "knew where there were manual records to check should questions arise about the accuracy of the computerized record."[5] But only detailed observations could determine how often such checks actually took place. Similar observations could be made at many points where the authors essentially report what they were told about the workings of these systems.

This is not to say that all information reported to field investigators on all subjects should be checked against corroborating sources before being reported. Taken literally, such an injunction would paralyze most field investigations. But the necessity of corroboration rises in relation to the degree of controversy associated with matters under discussion, to the physical and social distance of informants from these matters, and to their complexity. The problem is not just that high-level informants may lie, though indeed they may. Perhaps even more serious distortions arise where management informants are simply out of touch with day-to-day practice in their own organizations. We have direct experience, for example, of instances where the lower-level personnel who actually handle files regularly are either unwilling or unable to follow official policy on such matters as confidentiality. Westin and Baker may be entirely correct in their optimistic verdicts on these organizations. But their own account of

[3] Ibid., p. 26.
[4] Ibid.
[5] Ibid., pp. 262–63.

their methods does not warrant confidence that they could verify informants' reports on those important matters where distortions were most likely to occur.

But these difficulties concern us less than those which arise from the intellectual structure of the analysis. The main conclusion which their study offers to the questions which they were commissioned to answer, it seems to us, is summarized in the following statement:

> Going beyond the site-visit findings, our forecast of technological trends in the 1970s indicates that there is very little likelihood that new developments will drastically alter the way in which organizational goals, institutional limitations, and legal and social constraints shape the reception and use of new computer technology. We anticipate more flexible and reliable computer systems, and greater ease in carrying on data exchanges between computerized systems. It is the increase of feasibility of data sharing, and not any significant changes in either privacy or due-process interests, that will be the most important effect of advances in computer technology during the next eight years.[6]

It may well be that the actual conversion, around the year 1970, from manual to computerized personal-information services in these organizations brought no immediate losses to personal privacy. But here we feel that the authors and their collaborators have taken us the long way around the barn to answer a question of subsidiary interest. They seem to be saying, in this passage and other summary remarks, that the transition to computing represents simply a continuation of more far-reaching processes of social change. With this we would agree. But Westin and Baker make no serious effort to analyze these larger processes, or to identify the kind of society which they are creating. They seem content to conclude that the program of moderate reform outlined in *Privacy and Freedom* will suffice to respond to the social issues thrown up by these changes. Yet to take such a position without serious inquiry as to where these processes are leading is unsatisfying. It should be unsatisfying even to those who wish to defend the reformist approaches described above.

[6] Ibid., p. 342.

17 □ The Evolution of Surveillance

Thus the Westin and Baker study offers few clues to the fundamental directions of change in personal-data management. These questions can only be answered through understanding the dynamics of what we term "bureaucratic surveillance." In this view, the bulk of the demands for personal information in modern societies arise from the efforts of organizations to administer to each of many persons their precise "due," in terms of the organizational treatments they "deserve." The attractions of such fine-grained discrimination in organizational action—for both organizations and the public—engender a continuing flow of new and more efficient uses of personal data.

Thus personal information may be regarded as a sought-after "raw material" for organizational decision-making. But where are organizations most likely to seek these raw materials? What areas of previously private life are the most promising targets for new ventures in organizational surveillance?[1]

Much organizational interest in the details of people's private lives relates to the effort to curtail one or another form of deviant behavior. Credit systems serve largely to coun-

[1] Points in the following discussion are developed more fully in James B. Rule, *Private Lives and Public Surveillance* (New York: Schocken, 1974), especially Chapter 8.

teract disruptive effects from those unwilling or unable to pay; police record systems serve to aid the control of crime and criminals. Thus new forms of surveillance are especially likely where they promise to enable organizations to root out some troublesome form of misbehavior. Innovations in surveillance which promise to identify potential shoplifters to department stores or terrorists to airlines or illegal aliens to immigration authorities, then, are bound to attract intense interest from the organizations involved.

But the nature of deviant activity may be only indirectly related to the personal data sought for its control. This makes it especially difficult to foretell what forms of personal information are most likely to come into demand. Where organizations take the record of past deviant behavior to predict future propensities for such behavior, the link is clear enough. No one is surprised that the police use criminal records from the past to anticipate and act against future criminality. But organizations also seek to predict the future behavior of those with whom they deal by studying nonintuitive statistical correlates of such behavior. Thus, if the IRS came to suspect that tax evasion was highly associated with venereal disease, that agency would probably seek the sweeping power to delve through people's medical records that it now enjoys relative to their bank accounts. One ought not to smile too quickly at this seemingly farfetched example. Social science research as turned up associations no less improbable than this. And when a given form of deviant behavior offends particularly powerful interests, the efforts to seek out information on its possible correlates may become intense.

But the interest in controlling deviant behavior is not the only occasion for the extension of bureaucratic surveillance. Many efforts to document details of private lives arise in an attempt to document and define what one might term fine-grained bureaucratic obligations. The enormous amounts of personal documentation required for medical insurance and Social Security, for example, serve largely to establish eligibility for those services. The growing importance of these bureaucratically determined benefits is hardly less important in fueling the spread of surveillance than the effort to suppress deviance in the ordinary sense. The point is, both bureaucracies and the publics to which they respond expect exact distinctions to be drawn—between the guilty and the innocent, between those likely to prove guilty and those not so likely, between the eligible and the ineligible, and among different forms and degrees of eligibility among the same people over time. Where distinctions can be drawn in the treatments owing to different members of the public, we can expect efforts to document the bases for these distinctions and hence to render them grist for the mills of bureaucratic action.

In virtually all innovations in mass surveillance, the pressure of public demand plays an important part. We can point to few systems of collection and use of detailed personal information in America which are foisted on a wholly unwilling public simply for narrow bureaucratic purposes. On the contrary, people often want and even demand the fine-grained decision-making afforded by personal-data systems. Criminal-record systems could not exist without the demands of the great majority of the public for keeping rigorous track of criminals. Credit systems would be impossible without the considerable public enthusiasm for the comforts of easy, convenient credit. As Part I pointed out, people may feel that their privacy is threatened by the demands for personal information characteristic of the modern world; but they often seem willing enough to yield personal data in specific instances where desired services are at stake.

Indeed, available evidence suggests that people's desire to see "justice" done, in one way or another, accounts for much of the popular demand for extension of surveillance. People seek their own "just deserts," in terms of the credit privileges, insurance rates, tax liability, passport use, or whatever to which they feel themselves entitled. At the same time, the public also demands effective discriminations *against* welfare cheaters, poor credit risks, dangerous drivers, tax evaders, criminals and the like. And these discriminations in the treatment of persons by organizations can only be achieved by recourse to personal-data keeping. The instinct of demanding "justice" in the allocation of scarce resources is of course as old as social life itself. But the capabilities of modern organizations have made it possible for organizations to apply such principles in decision-making relations with literally millions of persons.

Often it is difficult to say whether popular demands represent the cause or the effect of the growing sophistication of organizations in surveillance and control. The result, in either event, is more and more bureaucratic attention to and demand for such information. Thus we confess deep doubt about observations such as the following by Alan Westin:

> A close survey of the positions adopted by leading ideological and civic groups toward issues of surveillance and privacy since 1945 indicates that there is now a general identification of privacy with liberty, and that concern over unlimited governmental or private surveillance runs the ideological spectrum from the Daughters of the American Revolution to the New Student Left, and from the *National Review* to the *Nation*. . . . The cry that "Big Brother is Watching" is now raised by any person or group protesting against what he or it considers unfair surveillance. . . . Anxious articles and editorials about restoring norms of privacy have appeared in business, labor, legal and academic journals, and many civic groups have adopted policy resolutions deploring erosions of privacy.[2]

It all sounds good. No one is likely to come out *against* privacy. But a close look at the clamor for more of it suggests that its proponents do not all have the same thing in mind. The Daughters of the American Revolution may well deplore, let us say, government snooping into the tax-exempt status of conservative "educational" organizations. But they are likely to be first to demand more vigorous invasion of the privacy of groups like "the New Student Left." Journals like *The Nation* may well deplore invasions of the privacy, for example, of welfare mothers, but be quick to support FBI investigation of right-wing militant groups.

People do protest what they consider "unfair surveillance"—often in the same breath with which they demand more vigorous surveillance for purposes which they support. Nearly all people can point to some form of surveillance with which they are unhappy, either because they disapprove of the ends at which it is directed, or because it is inefficient in the pursuit of these ends. But most people remain quick to

[2] Alan F. Westin *Privacy and Freedom* (New York: Atheneum, 1967), p. 378.

demand surveillance, whenever it seems to promise effective pursuit of ends which they deem desirable. Public and private bureaucracies are usually only too willing to accommodate these demands, where indeed they have not encouraged them to begin with. And the long-term effect can only be further pressure against personal privacy, in the sense in which most people use that term.

There seems no natural limit to the growth of surveillance. That is, there is no form of personal information which might not, under certain conditions, come to serve the purposes of formal organizations aiming at some form of social control. Such forms of control may be brutal or humane; they may be instituted autocratically or with the widest popular participation. But so long as the efficiency criterion continues in force, the potential for extension of surveillance to more and more areas of life is endless. The theoretical end point of such trends is a world in which every thought and action of everyone registers at once with a centralized monitoring agency.[3] To point to such an extreme is scarcely to announce its imminent attainment; but the significance of this theoretical end point for present developments bears reflection nonetheless.

Certainly no area of human life is inherently too private to attract the application of bureaucratic surveillance. Indeed, the most sensitive and "personal" aspects of life are often most associated with the social uncertainties which make systematic monitoring and control attractive. People yield all sorts of embarrassing or otherwise sensitive information to medical personnel as one of the costs of modern medical care. They provide nearly as sensitive information to insurance companies when filing claims for reimbursement for such care. As correlations are established between particular kinds of personal data and new possibilities for social control, demands for the data in question are sure to follow.

Growth of modern surveillance practices has already brought about unprecedented intimacy between large organizations and ordinary people. This distinctive closeness between bureaucracies and individuals is full of implications for the powers of these bureaucracies. The ability to know each

[3] For more detailed discussion of these issues, see Rule, *Private Lives and Public Surveillance,* especially Chapter 9.

person, and to act forcefully where that person is concerned, confers considerable power on the organization. The growth of this power represents a major condition of the rise of the modern state. Yet the power seems so natural in our own era that we take it for granted.

Any comparison to the closest sociological equivalents to modern social systems quickly underlines these differences. As Richard N. Adams has noted, writing about ancient empires,

> In centralized empires, as in the African segmentary states, the king or emperor had relatively little real control over the more distant and peripheral areas. The famous Spanish colonial refrain of "I obey but do not comply" was an expression of the fact that the king was indeed many months away, and his orders could be shelved or ignored for extended periods. The "colony" had to produce certain things for the mother state, but slowness of communication and transport meant that the local delegated agents of the crown were locally more important than the crown itself. Karl W. Deutsch has observed that "The basis of empires is the political apathy of most of their populations," an observation indicating that empires relied more on the weakness of the ruled than on the strength of the rulers.[4]

The apathy of these populations, of course, arose from the relative absence of direct interaction between them and the central powers. The decision of those at the center to launch a new war or to impose a new tax might have its effects eventually upon the more backward areas. But such direct ties between central powers and the general populace as those entailed, let us say, in a modern Social Security system would have been impossible in these ancient states.

[4] Richard N. Adams, *Energy and Structure: A Theory of Social Power* (Austin: University of Texas Press, 1975), p. 268.

18 □ The Limits of Surveillance and Control

Though the connection may seem improbable, the role of surveillance in the growth of modern social systems raises many of the same issues which concerned Thomas Hobbes in *Leviathan*. What forces, Hobbes wondered, accounted for people's willingness to fulfill distasteful social obligations? Why, for example, did people keep contracts, given the nearly universal temptation not to? Hobbes' explanation was people's fear of the overwhelming coercive power of the state. People meet burdensome civil obligations, he argued, simply because the punishments meted out by the state should they fail to do so are much more distasteful than the obligations themselves. Hobbes' conclusion was that even the most oppressive state was better than the anarchy which would surely reign without the threat of state coercion.

Today we live in a world much different from Hobbes'. Contractual relations are not nearly so problematic. Many aspects of modern social systems, including sophisticated forms of surveillance and social control, make it possible to contract even very complicated responsibilities over long periods of time. Presumably Hobbes would have been astounded at the level of compliance, say, with income taxation in present-day America. After all, people's assets often are not visible, nor is what they owe in taxes easily assessed. Yet people do pay. Undoubtedly these relatively high levels of compliance stem from taxpayers' awareness of IRS monitoring of countless sources of data relating to tax obligations. Moreover, the ability of the IRS to maintain contact with people virtually wherever they go in America surely enhances the effectiveness of this form of social control. The temptation to evade obligations in any particular year must be weighed against virtual certainty that this year's returns, or the absence of them, will be evaluated in conjunction with tax-relevant information monitored in subsequent years. By the same token, compliance with credit obligations, payment of parking and traffic citations, compliance with selective-service obligations, and a host of other more or less distasteful duties depend on well-organized surveillance and efficient social control.

Hobbes, perhaps because of personal experience of the English Civil War, set enormous store by the coercive force required to quell destructive pursuit of self-interest. In retrospect, he surely overestimated the sheer coercive power required, while little understanding the importance of mechanisms for monitoring human behavior and administering just the right sanctions at the right time. An occupying army may extort all the tribute which the traffic will bear from an enslaved people. But only a modern surveillance system can ensure the predictable payment of precisely the required amounts of income tax, year in and year out.

Hobbes saw anarchy as the scourge of civilized social life. He evidently felt that it was never far from the surface—hence his insistence on rigorous, even ruthless social control. But in the monolithic, centrally coordinated social systems of advanced industrial societies, many would perceive the opposite danger—that of excessive surveillance and control. Surely one can imagine too much of these essential social processes, just as one can imagine too little. At some point, rational consideration of the growth of sophisticated modern surveillance demands that such growth be deliberately limited.

Limited, not because such systems may be unfair, secret, or inefficient. Procedural reforms can at least in theory correct such deficiencies. But beyond a certain point, the development of bureaucratic surveillance must be regarded as an undesirable thing in itself. At some point, people find the attentions of really thoroughgoing surveillance simply too intrusive. And the social power which manifests itself in really effective, highly centralized systems becomes too awesome.

Consider the power issue. Virtually any social order offers some possibilities of domination—either within the family, within the community, or on a more sweeping scale. But the scope of repressive practices varies widely according to the form of social organization in which they occur. When social life is localized, when the *scale* of social relations is small, the numbers of persons affected by sweeping applications of power is at least limited. Life in the ancient political empires cited by Richard Adams may in many respects have been miserable by modern standards. But the remoteness of most people's daily lives from the reach of the central powers at least ensured a certain insulation from centralized political repression. Totalitarianism, the direct and relentless application of power from the center against every or nearly every member of society, is necessarily a modern phenomenon.

In more traditional social systems the lack of sophisticated technology and modern centralized forms of administration make it difficult for any single repressive agency to act against everyone or nearly everyone. Much of conservative political and social thought has arisen from anxieties about the centralization of power inherent in the modern nation-state. In these views, the growth of centralized political powers and the consequent superseding of local autonomies overturn desirable restraints. Attempts to distribute power through institutional checks and balances may be seen as efforts to compensate for the breakdown of such restraints.

In the growth of modern surveillance we see the social analog of the coalescence of centralized political power in the modern state. For whatever purposes originally govern the workings of these systems, they all provide the potential for centralized influence over individuals. Any system which enables authorities to monitor people's activities and respond to those activities with pertinent action embodies such repressive potential. Income-tax surveillance, for example, can become a means for monitoring and harassing those with uncongenial political views. Virtually the same holds true for surveillance systems associated with credit, insurance, social security, or any number of other well-monitored areas of modern life. Dramatic takeover of a nation's institutions by outside forces, as in the Nazi occupations, may provide the occasion for realizing these potentials. But sharp discontinuities are hardly necessary for such results. They may equally well arise through quiet political evolution and changes in power relations.

To be sure, the potential of modern social-control systems as instruments of repressive control may remain purely potential. The possibility that, let us say, income-tax surveillance may be used to track people's movements for political purposes may never become more than a possibility. But the fact that such things are possible introduces a new element in the life of modern societies.

Seen in this light, the notion of "balancing" the prerogatives of data-keeping organizations and those of individuals, or of "weighing" the demands of privacy and the need for information, seems superficial. Procedural reforms such as those discussed in Part II may provide a method for individuals to assert their interests in the uses of their personal documentation. But these safeguards are matters of social convention. They endure only as long as the political and social climate in which they arise. In a more profound sense, the "balance" between individuals and centralized organizations is permanently altered once these systems are in place. Certainly, where personal-data systems are indispensable, procedural safeguards are better than none at all. But it is misleading to argue that such safeguards somehow return the balance of social power to its status before the establishment of centralized institutions.

Bureaucratic structures have no *purposes* of their own. Formal organizations develop capabilities of doing certain kinds of things—of mastering given forms of uncertainty—but the ends which these skills serve are not dictated by the tools. A list of names and addresses, an array of pertinent information, or a bureaucratic mechanism for collecting and ordering such data—once in place, these resources exist for the benefit of whoever controls them. The purposes leading to the founding of such a system need not shape their continued working. Creating rules by which individuals are accorded a measure of control over "their" data is desirable in itself. But it has no effect beyond the point where all concerned cease playing by the rules.

A close look at modern American surveillance systems reveals many changes of function just within the last few decades. These changes—which mostly entail the assumption of new surveillance tasks—are all the more remarkable when one remembers that the systems themselves are relatively new. Part I noted, for example, how rapidly the American income-taxation system had developed since its inception in 1913; this rapid expansion has occurred both in the proportion of all Americans covered by the system and in amount of information demanded from each taxpayer. As the scope of IRS operations has widened, so have its exchanges of data with other organizations. Since the very beginning, income-tax data have been available to the Justice Department for use in prosecuting tax cases.[1] This, incidentally, includes use for litigation to which the individual who filed the return is not a party. Since the founding of the Social Security system in the 1930s, the IRS has been the instrument of collection of Social Security payroll taxes. The IRS also provides other personal data to Social Security in connection with administration of certain other benefits for which the latter is responsible. Since early in its life, the Internal Revenue Service has also cooperated with state and local taxation systems; since 1935, for example, state tax officials have been authorized to compare federal tax returns with state returns. Today, most states engage in joint auditing and other joint surveillance practices with the IRS. The Alcohol, Tobacco and Firearms Division, moreover, has always worked closely with state authorities in the pursuit of moonshiners and other tax violators. Finally, the President and the heads of other agencies have long been able to request tax information about those they claim to be prospective appointees to federal positions. Under this practice, for example, the Justice Department requested such information in 835 cases in 1974 regarding judicial nominees.[2]

One of the most noteworthy extensions of IRS surveillance is the development of the Parent Locator Service. Beginning

[1] John C. Chommie, *The Internal Revenue Service* (New York: Praeger 1970), pp. 169–72.

[2] Internal Revenue Service, *ADP in IRS*, p. 8; Chommie, *Internal Revenue Service*, pp. 163, 166; Privacy Protection Study Commission, *Citizen as Taxpayer*, Appendix 2 to *Personal Privacy in an Information Society* (Washington, D.C.: U.S. Government Printing Office, 1977), p. 15.

in 1967, the IRS made available to the states information on residence and employment of parents who had abandoned children to public support. This information served to aid state efforts to compel such parents to contribute to their children's support. Congress formalized and extended these arrangements in 1976 with legislation which authorizes the Federal Parent Locator Service to demand such information "from any . . . department, agency, or instrumentality, of the United States."[3] The only exceptions are made for national-security information and census data. In addition, the 1976 action makes IRS data available under certain circumstances "to parents, relatives and guardians of a child who is not being supported out of public funds and whose absent parent may not be the object of an outstanding support order."[4] Along with the Social Security Administration, the IRS is currently the chief source of residence and employment information for the PLS.

Similar transformations have shaped the development of Social Security. When the Social Security Board came into existence in 1935, much controversy surrounded the uses to which information gathered by the system might be put. Most of these controversies stemmed from fears that Social Security information might come to abet discrimination against pro-union workers by their employers. The board sought to allay these fears in statements issued in 1936, promising that only the worker himself, his immediate family, or government employees having official responsibility in connection with the files could get access to them. By 1949, in a departure from the original confidentiality rules, Social Security had begun to share information with other surveillance systems. Personal data were released in connection with national-security cases; in immigration-enforcement matters concerning aliens; and in cases involving federal income-tax laws. 1965 saw the passage of Medicare legislation, instituting a system now administered by Social Security and covering some 21 million Americans. In 1972, amendments to the Social Security Act included a provision to tighten up Social Security number issuance, requiring from each applicant proof

[3] Privacy Protection Study Commission, "Citizen as Taxpayer," p. 16.
[4] Ibid.

of age, identity, and citizenship in order to curtail welfare fraud and illegal immigration. Changes in the law governing private pension plans, in 1974, led to demands by private organizations (such as union pension funds) for Social Security data to supplement their own. The Social Security Administration agreed to such a disclosure, on the condition that the individual sign a consent form provided by the organization concerned. This disclosure raises privacy issues in that unions might be inclined to penalize workers whose records show they accepted nonunion employment. In 1975 a new amendment to the Social Security Act required that states use Social Security Administration data to check the eligibility of recipients of various state or locally administered public-assistance programs, such as Aid to Families of Dependent Children. And, of course, the establishment of the Parent Locator Service involved the Social Security Administration in very extensive surveillance whose purposes are unrelated to Social Security in the original sense.[5]

It is difficult to say for certain how these alterations in the uses of IRS and SSA data systems would have struck the founders of these systems. But given public concerns at the founding of these systems, and the history of popular opposition, say, to the Census, we suspect that some of these developments would have been considered unacceptable at the time of their beginnings. Yet the forces which led to the changes described above are easy enough to understand. In *Private Lives and Public Surveillance*, Rule noted the enormous pressures which develop for sharing the surveillance and control capabilities of any system which manages simply to remain in contact with very large numbers of people.[6] The development of any such system is so expensive, and the demand of centralized organizations to enforce obligations on members of the public so compelling, that the most vociferous efforts to keep the systems free of outside interference may not prevail. As one Social Security official put it,

> Build a better mouse trap, it has been suggested, and the world will beat a path to your door. The Social Se-

[5] Walter D. Rubinstein, "Confidentiality Under the Social Security Act," mimeo, Woodlawn, Md., Social Security Administration, 1975.

[6] James B. Rule, *Private Lives and Public Surveillance* (New York: Schocken, 1974); see especially "Symbiosis among Surveillance Systems," pp. 308–20.

> curity administration has built 2 (sic)—the social security number, which has been adopted to a great extent by government and private industry alike, and the heavily computerized social security data system. And, indeed, the world has begun to look to social security for the solution of problems which are far removed from the purpose of the program.[7]

Again, there need be no question of the sincerity of the intentions of the founders of these systems, or of the seriousness with which procedural safeguards are originally instated. The point is simply that political and social climates change, and that the inherent capabilities of organizational forms typically outlive the frame of mind of those who bring them into existence. David J. Seipp has found a remarkable quote from a spokesman for the FBI back in 1931. Asked whether the bureau would consider resorting to wiretapping, he replied,

> No sir. We have a very definite rule in the bureau that any employee engaging in wiretapping will be dismissed from the service of the bureau. . . . While it may not be illegal, I think it is unethical, and it is not permitted under the regulations by the Attorney General.[8]

The speaker was a young J. Edgar Hoover, replying to a query in a Congressional committee hearing.

Readers will differ in their attitudes toward the new uses which have emerged for the surveillance systems discussed above. Some will deplore the application of Social Security capabilities to the needs of the Parent Locator Serivce or the resort of the FBI to wiretapping, while others will applaud these things. But there is no doubt that changes in the purposes of surveillance can and do occur—often with dramatic and disastrous results. Perhaps the most drastic example was in the use of Dutch population records during the Nazi occupation to identify and track down Jews and other enemies of

[7] Rubinstein, "Confidentiality Under the Social Security Act," p. 23.
[8] U.S. Congress House of Representatives, Committee on Expenditures, *Wiretapping in Law Enforcement,* 71st Congress, 3rd Session, Hearings, 1931; quoted in David J. Seipp, *The Right to Privacy in American History*, Publication P-78-3, Program on Information Resources Policy, Harvard University, Cambridge, Mass., July 1978, p. 108.

the regime. This was a classical case of mobilization of a system created for the most mundane bureaucratic purposes for much different ends. One author who lived through this period has noted,

> Attacks by resistance fighters against population record offices were heroic feats to save people, as was the precision air raid carried out on 11 April 1944 by the 63rd RAF Squadron against the Kleykamp Art Gallery in The Hague, as a result of which 250,000 personal records were destroyed.[9]

Or consider an example much closer in time and space—the misuses of federal surveillance powers during the Nixon years. One of the most troubling trends of the Watergate period was the capture of IRS surveillance capabilities and their use for political purposes by the White House. The IRS monitored, for political purposes, both individual "enemies" and at least ninety-nine dissident political organizations during this period; the latter included not only obvious targets such as the Communist Party, but also Americans for Democratic Action and the Unitarian Society. In an effort to damage people and organizations labeled as political enemies, IRS data on them were forwarded to unfriendly agencies such as the CIA and the FBI. And yet, during the years before this period, many people would have considered it farfetched to suggest that such abuses could occur. Note, for example, the vigorous defense of official surveillance given in 1971 by William H. Rehnquist, then Assistant Attorney General, and later a Nixon appointee to the Supreme Court. Speaking for the Justice Department, he asserted that

> full utilization of advanced data processing techniques is by no means incompatible with the preservation of personal privacy. We reject the suggestion that the mere potential for abuse of these technological advances is a sufficient reason in itself to dispense with their use in the investigation and prosecution of crime. . . .
>
> I think it quite likely that self-discipline on the part of

[9] Frits W. Hondius, *Emerging Data Protection in Europe* (New York: American Elsevier, 1975), p. 187.

> the executive branch will provide an answer to virtually all of the legitimate complaints against excesses of information gathering.[10]

This statement was made, let us note, not long before the first Watergate crimes came to light.

By historical standards, the repressive trend in American government in the late 1960s and early 1970s represents a rather modest alteration in political climate. While harassment by IRS surveillance may have been disastrous to the people concerned, it at least occurred when opponents were vociferous and capable of fighting back. Had the repressive forces of this period succeeded in crushing the protest and in establishing a thoroughly totalitarian climate, the misuses of existing surveillance systems would surely have been much more serious.

But it has often been difficult even to convince people that such points are germane to the privacy issue. In 1975 the Federal Office of Telecommunications Policy commissioned a study of the privacy implications of electronic funds-transfer systems. These are arrangements in which people's accounts with banks and other financial institutions are maintained by computer and debited or credited electronically, without recourse to cash or paper. Perhaps the most interesting of these are "point of sale" facilities, in which people pay for goods or services by using a computer terminal in a place of business to debit the buyer's account, and credit the seller's, for the amount of the sale. The convenience of making such transactions without using cash, checks, or credit cards could make the use of such terminals as widespread as that of cash registers. The resulting net of personal-information exchange, however, could monitor users' movements and activities much of the time. And should use of these facilities grow as widespread as that of credit cards—something by no means impossible—this monitoring could well extend to the greater part of the adult population.

The resulting report, *Value Choices in Electronic Funds Transfer*, cited certain predictable controversies concerning access to data accumulated through the systems, security of

[10] Testimony before the Senate Judiciary Subcommittee on Constitutional Rights, 9 March 1971; quoted in *Congressional Quarterly, 1971 CQ Almanac*, p. 776.

transmission lines, and the like—well-precedented issues in recent writings on privacy.[11] But the report also raised some more fundamental questions about the possible uses of such systems for repressive purposes. How might a system of electronic funds transfer serve the intentions of some future totalitarian government? How readily could such a system serve to track politically dangerous persons for such a government? At what point do the capabilities of a system like this become so sweeping as simply to be better left untried?

These questions have occurred to others interested in electronic payment systems. In Congressional testimony given on June 23, 1975, the noted computer scientist Paul Armer expressed some similar misgivings about possible repressive uses of these systems. One of his more telling points went as follows:

> In 1971 a group of experts in computers, communication, and surveillance was assembled and given the following task: Suppose you are advisors to the head of KGB, the Soviet Secret Police. Further, suppose that you are given the assignment of designing a system for the surveillance of all citizens and visitors within the boundaries of the USSR. Further, the system is not to be too obtrusive or obvious. What was the group's decision? It was to build an EFTS system. Not only would it handle all the financial accounting and provide the statistics crucial to a centrally planned economy; it was the best surveillance system we could imagine within the constraint that it not be obtrusive.[12]

Similar reservations can be noted in a few other studies of EFT.[13]

[11] James B. Rule, *Value Choices in Electronic Funds Transfer Policy*, (Washington, D.C.: Office of Telecommunications Policy, 1975).

[12] At hearings held jointly by the Subcommittee on Constitutional Rights of the U.S. Senate Judiciary Committee and the Subcommittee on Science and Technology of the Senate Committee on Commerce.

[13] See, for example, Rob Kling, "Value Conflicts and Social Choice in Electronic Funds Transfer System Developments," *Communications of the Association for Computing Machinery*, Vol. 21, No. 8 (August 1978).

But most discussion of EFT planning has been among representatives of organizations, either government or private, with vested interests in such development. These writings have typically been either indifferent or downright hostile to consideration of the larger social implications of the systems. The Office of Telecommunications Policy report has been a focus of special annoyance among industry EFT planners. They are particularly unhappy with questions about the repressive potential of the systems they want to install. "Only the government could create [such repression]," several industry spokesmen have recently written, ". . . and whether or not it does so will hardly depend on whether EFTS is used for bill paying."[14]

We find such remarks unworthy of the larger social importance of the issue. Reasonable people may well disagree as to how to weigh the dangers associated with any particular surveillance practices. But no one can deny that, given a repressive political climate, the existence of central facilities for keeping track of people's whereabouts and activities must yield special advantages to those in power. Under such conditions one has no assurance whatsoever that private data will not become public property. Yet official planning for EFT, both by government and industry, has ignored these issues with a vengeance. The brief nod given to "protection of privacy" in the report of the federal EFT Commission is couched basically in the reformist terms discussed in Part II.[15]

We believe that virtually everyone would acknowledge some point at which surveillance by formal organizations simply becomes too thoroughgoing, even when carried out with total discretion for seemingly unimpeachable purposes. If electronic funds-transfer systems do not approach this point, one can always entertain still more thought-provoking examples. What if, instead of electronic funds transfer, someone were to propose a "wireless funds transfer" system, in which people were equipped with miniature radios, to be carried or worn at all times, and which were capable of authorizing deb-

[14] William F. Baxter, Paul H. Cootner, and Kenneth E. Scott, *Retail Banking in the Electronic Age* (Montclair, N.J.: Allanheld, Osmun and Company, 1977), p. 166. According to its preface, this work was initiated and funded by Citicorp, one of the biggest investors in EFT.

[15] National Commission on Electronic Fund Transfers, *EFT and the Public Interest* (Washington, D.C.: U.S. Government Printing Office, 1977), p. 29.

its from their accounts? Such a system would obviously offer even greater convenience than EFT, since one would always have total access to one's resources. But most people would begin to feel uneasy, we suspect, about any system which provided such intimate and potentially unerring contact between private persons and centralized powers.

Or, consider a medical-surveillance system designed to provide timely intelligence on threats to people's physical or mental health. Suppose that a tiny radio transmitter could be implanted under one's skin, to send continuous signals to a central computer for recording and monitoring. The cumulative record of such things as heartbeat, blood sugar, EEG, and the like could provide a data base for predicting all sorts of dangerous conditions, ranging from heart attacks to psychopathic outbursts. Indeed, if participation in the monitoring were required of everyone, medical research would certainly profit from the new source of data. Further, if the system embodied a way of pinpointing the location of each user, heart-attack victims and others involved in emergencies could count on prompt help. Continuous monitoring and analysis of data, under a system like this, could make it possible to transmit timely warnings, perhaps through the radio transmitter itself, to people in danger of ill health or antisocial impulses. From one point of view, a system like this would represent the ultimate in preventative care.

No one, we imagine, would find fault with the ultimate ends of such an undertaking—improving the quality of health care, and providing such care in the widest and most timely way. Nor would most people deny that collective institutions have an authentic interest in establishing control over the uncertainties of health. After all, the burdens of ill health invariably fall in one way or another on society as a whole. And there would be no insuperable difficulty in ensuring privacy in the conventional sense in a system like this. Procedural guarantees could well ensure such things as confidentiality, access rights, and due process in the use of data. And of course scrupulous efforts would have to be made to minimize intrusiveness.

But we suspect that none of these redeeming possibilities would make such an arrangement acceptable to most people, even if administered with the most scruplous guarantees and the best of motives. Such arrangements cause us to smile—or, if we take them seriously, to shudder—because they go too far in breaking down barriers which insulate individuals from larger institutions. Aesthetically, such arrangements revolt us because they would destroy the sense of aloneness and autonomy which most people count as essential ingredients of life. Strategically, the powers which such systems would confer on an overbearing regime are so sweeping that the risks of such misuse are simply better not taken. And even without repressive intent, the administration of such a system could hardly remain indefinitely free of pressures to share its capabilities for surveillance and control with other systems. The use of Social Security data for other purposes would be trivial compared to the demands made on systems like the ones imagined here.

But these are not the only grounds for objecting to the unlimited growth of surveillance. Such growth may also render social relations excessively "unforgiving" by preserving data on people's past misdeeds which might simply be better forgotten. All of these three considerations—the dangers of excessive concentrations of social power, the visceral revulsion at excessively intrusive monitoring, and the drawbacks of punishing people too severely for past misdeeds—may warrant curtailment of surveillance under some conditions. Nearly everyone would admit, at least in principle, that surveillance could go too far in any one of these respects. Stating a concern with these issues, however, is only a first step in the process of publicly weighing the drawbacks of these systems against the benefits which they offer. We do not wish to insist on any particular resolution of these choices for any particular system. But failure to acknowledge the urgency of these concerns is indefensible; and most of the standard writings and official statements on this subject have indeed failed in this respect.

The slow, incremental growth of surveillance systems blunts public awareness of the issues at stake. Systems of data collection are created with earnest guarantees; a few new items of data are added to the routine collections from time to time; occasional concessions are made to demands that the powers of the system be shared with other "legitimate" social interests—and none of these developments may strike anyone as disturbing in itself. Meanwhile, the official response to the privacy issue provides a way of helping people to live more easily in a world of encroaching surveillance.

For the official answers seem to offer something for everybody. For data-keeping organizations, the right to gather virtually whatever data they find useful; for subjects of recorded data, the right to know about and participate in the uses of "their" information. Yet in the longer run, more and more efficient uses for personal data are continually being found; hence, more and more "legitimate" reasons to demand such data. Where are we to stop the unending growth of such demands—and how do we do so? The answers to these questions will not be found in procedural reform.

19 □ The Alternative: A Looser, More Private World

We suspect that most people, confronted with these concerns, would hardly remain indifferent. No one really likes the idea of endless growth of bureaucratic surveillance; but what alternatives can there be?

That people find it difficult to conceive of realistic alternatives reflects the superficiality of most discussions of the privacy issue. A virtually universal assumption in these discussions is that of organizations' "needs" for personal data. This assumption becomes woven into a tenuous chain of logic which seems to go something like this: (1) The "needs" of bureaucracies for personal data are relentlessly rising; (2) the continued satisfaction of these needs is a condition for a more bountiful, more efficient, more "advanced" social world; so that (3) the only reasonable policy is to satisfy such needs while making organizational demands for data as fair and as palatable to the public as possible.[1]

[1] This statement of the argument is, of course, our paraphrase of many discussions on the subject. See, for example, Privacy Protection Study Commission, *Personal Privacy in an Information Society* (Washington, D.C.: U.S. Government Printing Office, 1977), pp. 5–6; or Westin, Alan F. *Computers, Health Records and Citizen Rights* (Washington, D.C.: U.S. Government Printing Office, 1976), p. 271.

Obviously we share the view that modern formal organizations benefit from use of personal documentation. But the lock-step argument above caricatures the thoughtful analysis of this reliance which the issue requires. The argument sets up a false choice between increasing loss of personal information to bureaucratic surveillance and a return to some sort of organizational Stone Age. But in fact the "needs" of organizations for personal information are hardly a *sine qua non* of organizational life. The alternatives to ever increasing use of personal data have not received the attention which they deserve.

Organizations collect personal information to make decisions about people. Better data means more accurate discriminations among the people with whom organizations must deal—hence better decisions, from the viewpoint of the organization. But which decisions are "better" or "worse" is a matter which might well be reconsidered in the interests of protecting privacy. If organizations were not expected to make such highly refined distinctions between people, the need for rigorous data collection would be greatly eased. *The alternative to endless erosion of personal privacy through increased surveillance is for organizations to relax the discriminations which they seek to make in their treatment of people.*

Today organizations, both governmental and private, invest enormous resources in pursuing these fine discriminations. We propose a reallocation of resources toward less discriminatory, less "information-intensive" ways of dealing with people. What we face here is not simply a choice between meeting the "information needs" of organizations and seeing these organizations grind to a halt. The choice is between the costs of discriminating and the costs of relaxing such discrimination. For every degree of intimacy of surveillance relinquished by organizations, benefits accrue in privacy and autonomy.

Pursuit of less information-intensive alternatives would entail fundamental change in people's expectations of organizations. It would mean minimizing differences in how people are treated in light of their "records," and hence minimizing the necessity for developing such records. Instead of sharpening their discriminations, organizations would be expected to provide a "baseline" of adequate resources for all, with minimal differences between cases.

Income taxation provides a good example of the range of choices involved. From its relatively simple beginnings, the U.S. income-tax system has become a giant consumer of personal data. The rise in the amount of data collected corresponds directly to the growing number of personal circumstances which tax laws take into account in assessing liability. A major impetus for such growth, one supposes, is public demand for "just consideration" of various extenuating circumstances. But simpler tax laws might well aim at limiting the range of circumstances bearing on tax obligations. If discriminations were made less complicated, then demands for personal information would drop commensurately. Planners for tax reform could make an enormous contribution to privacy protection by cutting back the range of personal data which bear on tax liability.

A relatively easy avenue for seeking less information-intensive forms of bureaucratic action lies in those areas where the use of personal information is least cost-effective. One of the most intrusive bureaucratic demands now widespread in America is that associated with security clearances. Millions of persons must routinely undergo such investigations as conditions of employment. Yet to our knowledge, high correlations between the results of these investigations and, let us say, unauthorized leaks of security-related information have never been demonstrated. We suspect that the "information needs" attributed to our security apparatus in these respects are simply exaggerated. Such an examination would more likely show that whatever benefits such procedures yield do not nearly warrant the costs in loss of privacy.

It is easy to attack demands on personal privacy which do not really benefit organizations, however. Nearly all writers on the subject have done so. The difficult cases lie where organizational use of personal information is both useful to organizations and destructive of privacy. Here serious consideration of the arguments put forward above demands forswearing bureaucratically attractive uses of personal data. This would mean setting policies in which organizations would relax or abandon the single-minded pursuit of efficient discrimination among persons in favor of other considerations.

No doubt it is easiest to apply this thinking in the planning for bureaucratic systems which do not yet exist. The prospect of National Health Insurance, for example, is receiving increasingly serious discussion at the time of this writing. The potential of such systems for invading privacy is obviously vast. In particular, systems which embody complicated eligibility requirements and other forms of discrimination governing access to treatment are driven to make very intensive demands on personal data. But if the system offered its services to all, as in Britain's National Health Service, it need not develop the detailed inquiries into the backgrounds of its clients which complex eligibility criteria require. The British system actually entails relatively loose central record-keeping. What there is serves mainly to keep track of the numbers of patients for whom individual physicians are responsible. Case histories and other strictly medical information are stored locally, much as they are in countries where medicine is private.

One can also envisage ways to enhance privacy by restricting surveillance where it is already well established, although resistance would be greater here. Consider the case of consumer credit. The first consumer-credit-reporting operations were simply listings of bad debts held in common among several firms, to enable each to avoid giving credit to persons who had defaulted elsewhere. Today, by contrast, credit surveillance entails use of a very wide variety of information pooled among many different sources. The sophistication of modern credit systems depends on the use of this detailed information to predict which credit applicants should be trusted, and to what extent. The interests of privacy would be well served by deliberately blunting some of these discriminations.

This possibility has not gone altogether unnoticed among writers on privacy. Kent Greenawalt, in his thoughtful study of the status of privacy in American law, has commented,

> If information about credit standing is easily available on a national basis, it is virtually impossible to avoid one's low credit rating. This information allows credit-granting agencies to make more intelligent decisions about risk, but is it socially desirable that persons who admittedly pose a high risk be unable to get credit? Perhaps it would be socially preferable if credit were more

> freely available, even if good credit risks ended up paying the tab (e.g., in increased prices) so that poor credit risks could get credit.[2]

Nonetheless, Greenawalt's remarks are exceptional; as Part II pointed out, most writers have taken the sacredness of the efficiency criterion for granted.

We share Greenawalt's view. The effectiveness of discriminations between good and poor credit risks is hardly the only social value which ought to be considered in this important relationship. Competing values here are those of a looser social world, one with less potential for serving the needs of oppressive centralized powers and more capacity for extending opportunities to those who, in light of "all the facts," may appear to be poor risks. We favor a commitment of resources to pursuit of these latter goals. Any number of concrete measures, more or less sweeping, might achieve this. One might restrict the retention of derogatory credit information to, let us say, two years. This would have the effect of wiping the slate clean after a relatively short period for those who have been unwilling or unable to pay in the past. Or one might do away with centralized credit reporting altogether, so that every firm extending credit would have to develop its own basis for deciding whether to open an account with a given applicant.[3] This would moderate the intrusive character of modern credit investigations. Our point is not to argue for any particular measure, but rather to emphasize that there are alternatives to the narrow pursuit of efficient decision-making which characterizes current credit policy. Whether the resulting policies are sweeping or moderate matters less than recognizing that protection of privacy requires compromises in bureaucratic efficiency.

Another common relationship between individuals and formal organizations which relies heavily on surveillance is auto insurance. Insurance firms believe that people with bad

[2] Kent Greenawalt, *Legal Protections of Privacy* (Washington, D.C.: Office of Telecommunications Policy, 1975), p. 92.

[3] To the consternation of the credit-reporting industry, certain large credit grantors, mostly petroleum companies, are developing systems to evaluate applicants' credit worthiness without recourse to centralized credit files. Moreover, they are refusing to disclose information about accounts to credit bureaus.

reputations fare less well in litigation than others. Wishing to avoid heavy court judgments against people they insure, companies either decline business from persons reported to be disreputable, or accept it at higher rates than otherwise. Thus the interests of the companies in efficient discrimination, implemented through sophisticated surveillance, serve to reinforce the effects of community prejudice.

Less information-intensive, less discriminatory approaches could very well replace practices like these. Such a replacement would scarcely affect the viability of insurance systems. It would, however, make the entire community, rather than a few individuals, bear the cost of the community's prejudices. Quite apart from any of the other arguments for such a redistribution, it would remove the necessity for some particularly invasive forms of surveillance.

Ideas like this are not wholly unprecedented. In a statement published at the end of 1977, James M. Stone, then Commissioner of Insurance for the state of Massachusetts, questions the desirability of many forms of insurance surveillance. After noting the hypothetical advantages to insurance companies of collecting data on applicants' "emotional makeup, reaction under stress, use of alcohol and the status of the driver's marriage," he comments,

> The dangers to society of information gathering for improved classification accuracy must be weighed against the benefits of higher predictive ability in the system. The danger of classifying based on the kind of variables described above should be obvious. On some of the possibly useful variables, the Constitution or legislative bodies have spoken with finality. Others are presumably unused because someone in the insurance industry has enough foresight to anticipate the hostile public reaction their introduction would invite. It would take a strong argument to convince me that any possible benefit from upgraded predictive accuracy could outweigh the harm of sanctioning insurers to invade each policyholder's private life.[4]

[4] "Opinions, Findings and Decisions on 1978 Automobile Insurance Rates," Commonwealth of Massachusetts, Division of Insurance, 28 December 1977, pp. 148–49.

Stone's argument, developed at considerable length, attacks some of the central assumptions of current insurance practice in America.[5] His statement has met with consternation from insurance companies themselves.

The administration of welfare and other social services is another area in which privacy is invaded. There are stringent eligibility requirements for nearly all forms of public welfare, unemployment benefits, and public disability insurance. These requirements necessitate close surveillance of recipients' lives, ranging from requirements of personal documentation to unannounced visits to recipients' homes.[6] Many writers have noted that welfare bureaucracies use these information requirements as punitive devices, to make it as unpleasant as possible for people to obtain welfare.[7] No one, to our knowledge, has been willing openly to defend these intrusive practices as good things in themselves. But the logic of the situation—shortage of resources, overlapping jurisdictions among organizations, and stringent limits on eligibility—foster demands for detailed personal information.

The less information-intensive alternative here would be to establish a "floor" under all incomes, regardless of eligibility criteria. There are elements of this thinking in proposals for a negative income tax or a guaranteed family income. By making nearly everyone eligible for a basic level of support, the need for surveillance could be greatly reduced. Welfare reform is now undergoing serious discussion throughout the United States, and one of the key options under discussion is federalization of all state and county welfare programs. If the harm done to privacy by present welfare systems is taken

[5] Though central, such assumptions are not necessarily uniform among all insurance companies and all forms of insurance. One of the few major trends in relations between bureaucracies and mass publics which seems to counterval *against* the growth of surveillance is the reliance on group rather than individual insurance policies. In the former, rates are assessed according to characteristics of the group, so that the incentive for surveillance over individuals is absent.

[6] See, for example, the thoughtful discussion of these issues in Joel F. Handler and Margaret K. Rosenheim, "Privacy in Welfare: Public Assistance and Juvenile Justice," *Law and Contemporary Problems*, Vol. 31, No. 2, Spring 1966.

[7] Frances Fox Piven and Richard A. Cloward, *Regulating the Poor: The Functions of Public Welfare* (New York: Vintage Books, 1971), pp. 154–55.

seriously, then planners will surely want to consider less discriminatory alternatives of this kind.

These less information-intensive alternatives would hardly be free of cost. In auto insurance, curtailing use of information on people's reputations would in effect redistribute the costs of community prejudice to the community as a whole. In credit, relaxing discriminations based on surveillance would raise the cost of credit to "good" credit risks unless credit grantors were made to accept these costs themselves. In social services, the public would bear the costs of providing more freely resources which are now dispersed only on a highly discriminatory basis. The extent of the costs, in each case, would depend on the extent to which discriminations were relaxed. These costs, in turn, would be mitigated to varying degrees by the savings which would result from reducing expensive surveillance. In any event, it should be clear that the choice is not between the most relentless possible discrimination and none at all. Instead, it is one of how much privacy we are prepared to buy, at a cost of incremental losses in efficiency.

Another kind of cost which would result from relaxing surveillance efforts would be symbolic rather than financial. Much public support for surveillance no doubt stems from the perception that such practices are directed against certain unpopular groups—welfare cheaters, bad credit risks, tax evaders, and political dissidents, for example. Those who identify themselves as "respectable" members of society are quick to support measures directed against such "unrespectable" elements. Elites have often encouraged such reactions, emphasizing status distinctions between "respectable" benefits such as unemployment insurance and Social Security and "unrespectable" benefits such as welfare.[8] Under these conditions, those who consider themselves "respectable" might deplore a lessening of enforcement activities which they see as distinguishing them from the unrespectable.

Still, precedent does exist for alternatives to relentless pursuit of bureaucratic discrimination in the treatments accorded to people. It has long been believed in the consumer-credit industry, for example, that blacks are poorer credit risks than whites—even with allowance for the fact that blacks as a

[8] See Lawrence M. Friedman, "Social Welfare Legislation: An Introduction," *Stanford Law Review*, Vol. 21, January 1969, pp. 217–47.

category have less education and lower incomes than whites. This supposition, it appears, may have some factual basis; the history of antagonism between black communities and local merchants could well account for such a trend.[9] In any event, many credit grantors long believed in this association, and discriminated accordingly against blacks in their credit policies. Under the Equal Credit Opportunity Act, however, such discrimination is now unlawful. The reason for the passage of the act, one assumes, was not any question over the efficiency of the criterion for bureaucratic purposes, but rather the feeling that the moral and social costs of maintaining this discrimination are simply too high.

Another instance in which efficiency in surveillance has thus far been sacrificed to other values is in requirements for standard identification documents for American citizens. Many European countries have long required identity cards which amount to domestic passports. Such a system would greatly facilitate law-enforcement activities in America on a variety of fronts, including control of illegal aliens, identification of criminal suspects, and counterespionage. In fact, official identification is now demanded so frequently from so many Americans that, as noted earlier, the driving license approaches serving as an all-purpose identity card. But federal authorities have avoided any overt move in the direction of identity card systems *per se*. There has recently been discussion of devising a tamperproof Social Security card, mainly to counteract the hiring of illegal aliens, but federal officials have apparently judged that a full-scale system of federally required, rigorous personal identification would be politically unacceptable. Their judgment is prudent. Most Americans seem not to like the idea of having to carry "papers" simply on general principles—unless there are tangible advantages to doing so, as with credit cards. When certain Justice Department officials proposed such a program to Congress in 1975, the idea was later repudiated by the Attorney General.[10]

Rumblings from the Executive Branch and Congress at the time of this writing continue to suggest high-level reluctance to accept responsibility for initiating new federal surveillance ca-

[9] See David Caplovitz, *The Poor Pay More* (Glencoe, Ill.: Free Press, 1963).

[10] See the *New York Times* stories on the proposal and its subsequent reversal on 4 February 1975 and 4 April 1975.

pabilities. In January 1978, the Carter administration ordered curtailment of an IRS computer system which, in the words of one report, "would have given 48,300 internal revenue agents almost instantaneous access to the tax returns of all individual and corporate taxpayers."[11] Similarly, plans for extending the role of the FBI in providing surveillance data to state and local law enforcement authorities have run into repeated opposition. Conflicts have developed with both the Ford and Carter administrations over the FBI system. The Carter administration at first decided to continue the project, only to order another halt in the face of Congressional opposition.[12] A newspaper story on some related developments quoted Senator Edmund Muskie as saying, "While some may not view this as an efficient course, such Government 'inefficiencies' often provide us with the only safeguard of our liberty."[13]

Beneath the political infighting and the inability of public figures to take a coherent position, there is intellectual confusion. Most people experience deep reservations about unlimited growth in the surveillance powers of centralized agencies. Under some conditions, even those in positions of power may come to share these reservations. This is especially likely when the growth of surveillance occurs in the full glare of critical public attention, or when top officials fear that powers of an agency like the FBI may ultimately be used against people like themselves. But commitment to bureaucratic efficiency runs very deep in our culture. Public figures find it difficult to accept *deliberate* limitation of admittedly efficient data-management practices. Senator Muskie's statement, though obviously true, is not yet a firm basis for a programmatic, politically attractive approach to surveillance policy. Thus the frequent recourse to justify positions like his with objections to the "abuse" or inefficiency of data systems—shortcomings which surveillance proponents are only too willing to correct.

Nonetheless, as these examples show, the efficiency criterion for guidance of personal-data management does not

[11] David Burnham "The Watch on Computer Privacy," *New York Times*, 15 January 1978, p. E7.

[12] David Burnham, "F.B.I. Data Network Poses Privacy Issue," *New York Times*, 17 July 1978.

[13] quoted in Burnham, "The Watch on Computer Privacy," p. A10.

reign absolutely supreme. People do value looser, less discriminatory, less information-intensive alternatives in many settings, and policy-makers have occasionally accommodated these attitudes. But these accommodations have usually been ambivalent. What is needed is a coherent justification for limiting bureaucratic efficiency to preserve privacy. Right now, the fate of any particular policy or program is less important than the principles involved in decisions about them. People must acknowledge that protection of privacy, autonomy, and a measure of desirable "looseness" in social life is incompatible with the unlimited growth of surveillance. Where personal-data management is deemed worth the drawbacks, rules of access, publicity, and due process are of course indispensable. Planning for such safeguards becomes unacceptable only when offered as a substitute for inquiring whether surveillance activities are worth having in the first place.

It is ironic that these arguments are often dismissed as radical or utopian. The radical forces are those pressing for more and more surveillance. Though often bracketed simply as technological innovations, these changes are actually reshaping key social relationships. Those concerned with preserving privacy, autonomy, and diversity in social life must seek alternatives to such changes—whether they consider themselves radicals, moderates, or conservatives. The alternative is to abandon the field to forces drawing us precipitately toward radical and unexamined changes, concealed in the Trojan horse of "business as usual."

Another key defense against taking our proposals seriously is that the changes concerned would be too costly. America, it is said, cannot *afford* a less efficient consumer-credit system, or more openhanded distribution of social services, or the curtailment of electronic funds-transfer systems. But these arguments are unconvincing on the face of them. They are most patently absurd where less information-intensive approaches would mean either preventing the development of systems which do not already exist, or returning existing systems to a point at which they recently flourished. We get along quite adequately without EFT at present, for example; indeed, the press for its institution comes from financial and government institutions, not from consumers. Why such systems need to be developed for a basically indifferent public is far from clear. Similarly, meaningful limitations on the use of personal data in credit decision-making need only entail returning these institutions to their state of a few decades ago. A less thoroughgoing credit-surveillance system would be less convenient and more costly, but it could still leave America with a much wider array of consumer-credit opportunities than are found in nearly any other country.

Again, seeking alternatives to the present drift toward more and more surveillance is not an easy course. It would entail costs—none of them more painful than those of revising long-accepted assumptions. But these costs should be considered in light of the broadest historical needs and choices confronting Americans today. What do we need more—more bureaucratic efficiency and closer social control, or greater privacy and more "looseness" in social relationships? In perhaps the most efficient bureaucratic society the world has known, it is difficult to consider the requirement for more such efficiency all-important. And in a society of unprecedented affluence, it is difficult to credit the notion that the financial costs of relaxed surveillance are unacceptable. But if these values are not in danger, those of privacy and autonomy certainly are. Surely our relatively efficient and affluent society ought to accept the costs of serious efforts at privacy protection.

PART IV

Reasoned Choice and the Future of Human Control

The emergence of the privacy issue and its assimilation in American policy thinking hold significance well beyond the issue itself. The growing ability of formal organizations to collect and use personal data for social control parallels other trends in highly developed societies. The social control arising from surveillance is analogous to the growing human control over the natural world. Is there any hope for exercising rational guidance over these powers of control?

20 □ "Rational" Planning

Reading of the unfolding controversies over personal-data systems, most readers have no doubt felt sense of *déjà vu*. This feeling, we think, is not illusory. Many public issues have their origins in practices which grow up gradually and almost accidentally. Such practices then, in their more developed forms, come to arouse anxieties. The last ten years, for example, have seen controversies over the effects of aerosols in the atmosphere, the role of nuclear power as an energy source, the effects of high energy consumption in general, the use of pesticides, and a long list of other points. What they have in common is the focusing of critical attention on the progressive results of what originally seemed unexceptionable, even banal choices. The ensuing controversies lead one to wonder whether reasoned planning can resolve the complicated social choices faced by highly developed societies.

The unfolding of the privacy issue exhibits many of these features. The development of personal-data systems in general, and of bureaucratic surveillance in particular, have occurred gradually. Organizations have adopted these practices on an *ad hoc* basis, to solve specific practical problems. In time, these discrete solutions to various management problems fuse into larger systems. As conditions change, organizations place increasing demands on the systems. After a time, the systems are so elaborate that people find it difficult to imagine how they could get along without them. And this applies both to the officials who manage the systems and to the publics who, in one way or another, become inured to the services they make possible.

Now that these systems are established, their sophisticated effectiveness has begun to arouse concern. The expression of this concern given in this book, of course, is very much a minority opinion. True, public-opinion studies have shown that Americans do experience a loss of privacy and identify bureaucratic data-management practices as at least partly responsible for such losses.[1] Yet any suggestion for seriously limiting the data demands of these systems meets with indignation. After all, it is said, no one has forced the public to accept such systems. Existing personal-data systems must represent expressions of people's "choice." The fact that people fill out their income-tax forms, apply for consumer credit, or submit to the questioning associated with insurance investigations is held to demonstrate popular acceptance of the systems which make these demands.

But these developments scarcely reflect choice in any meaningful sense. "Choosing" to acquiesce to the demands of a record-keeping bureaucracy may be no more meaningful than a worker's "choosing" to accept the wage offer of the only factory in town. Where requisite services are available only through yielding personal data, acceptance of distasteful conditions hardly implies approval of them.[2]

The notion of choice, either collective or individual, can have little significance without consideration of the range of alternative involved. People who confront surveillance requirements in seeking insurance, credit, or welfare do not

[1] For example, in our own study of 291 Long Island residents in 1976–77, 182 respondents (62 percent) felt that the use of computers had affected personal privacy in America. Of these, 142 (78 percent) saw the effects as negative.

[2] For example, in our study of Long Island residents, among the 144 of those sampled who agreed with the statement "Putting records on people in computers is a threat to freedom," only 10, or about 7 percent, reported ever having declined to seek some specific service or opportunity because of not wishing to provide information in their own right. Of those 67 respondents who reported that they objected to providing six or more particular items of personal information on a list provided in the questionnaire, only about 7, or about 10 percent, reported not applying for service for this reason.

choose, let us say, between more and less information-intensive approaches to these situations. They choose between cooperation with what seem routine though perhaps slightly disturbing demands, and foregoing the service in question. Often, of course, these are services which people cannot realistically go without.

The range of meaningful choice might well be extended, in cases like these, if demands for personal information were set in something like collective bargaining. In such an arrangement, representatives of data-using organizations would confront representatives of all providers of data on more or less equal terms. There, at least, the providers of data would not experience the obvious strategic disadvantages which stem from acting in isolation from one another. But such bargaining would still leave no room for reasoned reflection as to how the surveillance system came to "need" the data presently required to provide key services. Both in personal-data management and in other modern bureaucratic practices, the status of present arrangements as "rational" social choices has come very much into question.

The classic case is the role of the automobile in modern consumer societies. Today, practically no one professes satisfaction with the way in which the automobile has been assimilated in America's total transport arrangements. Cars and other highway transit manage to combine pollution with high energy use; yet a fraction of the capital invested in producing automobiles and providing amenities for them could have produced superior results in other forms of transit. This is not to say that anyone would have preferred to forgo automobile production altogether, given the choice, nor to suggest that people could easily agree on the alternatives which they might prefer to our present overwhelming reliance on cars. But few would deny that, if we could do it all over again, we would wish to alter our heavy dependence on private cars.

Clearly the unhappy present state of transport represents the results of "choice," in one sense of that term. At countless points in the development of the present situation, people have assessed the available alternatives in their own lives, scratched their heads, and decided to purchase a car, to buy a second car, or to plan for more highways. Yet the overall result could not be said to be "planned." People may well not have been content with the personal choices available to them, and no one was even remotely in the position of choosing—let us say, fifty years ago—between the present situation and a meaningful alternative. Both the advance knowledge and—no less important—the social structures to make such choice meaningful were lacking when fateful early decisions were made.

A catastrophic "run" on a bank, a panic in a crowded space, a traffic jam resulting from the breakdown of a light at a key intersection—all these situations reflect the cumulative results of many individual "choices." None of these results would have been the outcome of reasoned deliberation well in advance. But social life offers countless instances where the structures which might have provided the setting for more balanced, more "rational" consideration simply never exist—or do not exist until the opportunity for the decision has passed. Concerning both surveillance and other weighty social issues, the conscientious critic must try to create the intellectual and social structures for such decision-making before it is too late.

Ideally, in planning for major social changes, all interested parties could weigh all the alternatives before commitments were made to any one of them. Thus, in the case of automobile, one would have hoped for public discussion of the attractions and drawbacks of present arrangements to different groups *before* massive investments in cars and highways had been made. Of course, such far-seeing and disinterested public decision-making is a utopian prospect. But reasoned discussion ought to extend real debate over such issues as far as possible in this direction. In the case of surveillance and privacy, this means weighing alternatives which thus far have been denied largely by default.

Some would no doubt see such an appeal as reaching for the impossible. What we are seeking, it may be said, is clairvoyance. What major historical trend, from our growing reliance on the automobile back to the rise of industrialism itself, has been shaped by anything like full rational examination of all the major alternatives? Is it anything more than normal to find troublesome political and social realities emerging unexpectedly from the interaction of earlier individual plans and choices? Does not every generation have to do its best with the choices created by default in the previous generation?

Undoubtedly it is true that all sorts of social trends are in some sense "out of control" at any given moment. But this is hardly sufficient reason not to try to extend the scope of meaningful choice as far as possible. Financial planners do what they can—with mixed success, to be sure—to control national and international monetary affairs. Epidemiologists seek to halt the spread of serious diseases, often planning for eventualities which no one else might notice. Environmental specialists exert themselves to anticipate and combat long-term bad effects of practices which most people consider un- hardly sufficient reason not to try to extend the scope of these efforts and the countless others like them are fallible. They may succeed only in warning of dangers which do not materialize or, perhaps worse, of ones against which no corrective steps are possible. But to abandon such efforts on the grounds that they often fail would be taking pessimism to a suicidal extreme.

21 □ Planning as Ideology

Any approach to planning, however, must begin by assessing what can be changed and what can't be. Some elements of any planning situation, in other words, must be regarded as "fixed conditions," while others, with varying expenditures of resources, may be considered susceptible to change. Such calculations, however, are always riddled with political content.[1] For one thing, optimism about the possibility of change has long distinguished conservatives from progressives. Further, one is always tempted to believe that only what one *wants* to change *can* be changed. Thus, people readily designate those conditions whose change they would find uncongenial as "inherent in the nature of things"—just as they too readily assume the feasibility of changes which they most desire.

Discussion of the privacy issue, we have argued, has been marred by the assumption that the growing demands of surveillance systems must be regarded as fixed. This assumption has made it seem reasonable to interpret "the privacy problem" as a problem of helping people cope with more and more loss of personal data to bureaucracies. If the destination—a world of ever-increasing surveillance—is decided in

[1] For fuller discussion of this point, see James B. Rule, *Insight and Social Betterment: A Preface to Applied Social Science* (New York: Oxford University Press, 1978), especially Chapter 7.

advance, the only remaining question is how we wish to travel.

Occasionally official writings have suggested other possibilities. The report of the Privacy Protection Study Commission states, for example, states

> Whether or not the questions an organization asks individuals constitute intrusions on personal privacy is a problem that begins with the lines of inquiry society accepts as proper for an organization to pursue in making decisions about individuals. Thus, so long as society countenances a particular line of inquiry, questions as to how far it may properly go seem largely aesthetic. Indeed, if an individual's only concern is to be fairly treated, he should logically prefer to have recorded as much information as possible about himself as a protection against inaccurate evaluation.[2]

Here the Privacy Commission authors embrace one of the central arguments of this book—the notion that application of the efficiency criterion dictates ever-increasing demands for personal data. But their response to this realization is weak and equivocal. The question of how much intrusion into private lives is desirable or acceptable is not purely "aesthetic," if one considers the larger social implications of such demands. The closeness of bureaucratic monitoring afforded by the provision of information, and the implication of this closeness for power relations, go well beyond the aesthetic impact on individuals.

Perhaps more important, the commission writers display their political biases in deferring to "society" to limit the acceptability of organizational surveillance. "Society," of course, never acts in its own right. In this instance, Congress created the Privacy Commission specifically to provide advice on the guidance of personal-data policy. If under these circumstances the commission had no conclusion to offer, then it is unrealistic to expect "society" to offer one.

Throughout the Privacy Commission's report, and occasionally in other writings, a careful reader notes recognition

[2] Privacy Protection Study Commission, *Personal Privacy in an Information Society* (Washington, D.C.: U.S. Government Printing Office, 1977), p. 16.

of broader possibilities. By far the dominant tendency, however, is to assume that the relentless growth of bureaucratic surveillance is inevitable. Thus the commission authors write,

> We live, inescapably, in an "information society," and few of us have the option of avoiding relationships with record-keeping organizations. To do so is to forego not only credit but also insurance, employment, medical care, education, and all forms of government services to individuals.[3]

But as we noted in Part II, some conditions are more "inescapable" than others. There is nothing inherently impossible about reversing the demands of institutions for personal data; the conditions which make such a choice difficult are habits of thought and vested interests, especially among those close to the planning. There is no reason why a thorough review of the possibilities for privacy protection ought not to include consideration of curtailing the growth of surveillance.

Still, it is easy to identify the pressures which limit the alternatives considered by bodies like the Privacy Commission. The appointees to the commission included its chairman, managing partner of a large New York accounting firm; one liberal Congressman; one conservative Congressman; one official of the RAND Corporation; the head of one of the country's largest insurance companies; the former managing editor of a major urban daily newspaper; and one state senator and attorney. All of these people had won distinction in institutions attuned to the prevailing rhythms of American life; all, we may presume, had acquired reputations for combining shrewd stewardship of organizational interests with "social concern." Planners selected from such backgrounds are unlikely seriously to consider limitation of organizational efficiency or fundamental rearrangement of social advantage as approaches to privacy policy. Moreover, if such alternatives had ever been embodied in concrete recommendations, the political powers which were to act on the report would certainly not have welcomed them.

These institutional constraints, however, need not have applied to the independent scholars who have written on the

[3] Ibid., p. 5.

subject. Yet Westin, Miller, and others have shown if anything less sensitivity than the Privacy Commission authors to the possibility of fundamentally different approaches. One would have expected them to see the endless encroachment of "the information society" as something other than an immutable fact of life.

In any event, the pervasive influence exerted by the original interpretations of "the privacy issue" clearly demonstrates something about the constraints imposed by the idea of planning itself. Once established, the definition of fixed versus variable conditions is extremely difficult to change. And as we noted above, the definition typically embodies enormous partisan political content. Some writers have termed these usually unconscious constraints "the ideology of planning." By this they mean not the overt political program of planners, but the unacknowledged political content embodied in the very concepts of planning.

Examples come readily to mind. When authorities plan to deal with the "problem of slum housing," for example, they are apt to regard as a fixed condition of their planning the perpetuation of poverty and low purchasing power among those they aim to help. Or, planners dealing with "the mass-transport problem" take it for granted that the demands for freeways and the like will grow over coming decades as they have in the past. At best, such more or less unconscious constraints may be the price planners have to pay in order to be able to do *something*, even if they might really wish to do more. At worst, the ideology of planning may work to foreclose valuable choices. And the choices most in danger of being eliminated always seem to be those least congenial to elite interests.

A much-noted public-planning sequence which recently took place in Britain provides a perfect illustration. Planners had long agreed that a third major London airport would be required by the early 1980s, and both major political parties had endorsed this conclusion. Actually, those connected with aviation and transport planning had accepted this idea since World War II, assuming that the site would be Stanstead, in Essex. A major military airfield had been built there during the war, and by the 1960s it had been coverted to a low level of civilian use. The two existing major London airports, however, were by then judged to be approaching their capacity of use, and major upgrading was required if Stanstead was to become the third.

What the planners had not counted on, of course, was the vociferous opposition of those living near the proposed site. The prospective increase in air traffic, enlargement of the runways, and development of surface transport were all held intolerable, and a powerful lobby against siting the new facility at Stanstead quickly developed. By 1968 the Labour Party, long committed to the idea of the third airport but not necessarily to the Stanstead site, had come to power. The Labour government that year appointed a new commission, instructed "to inquire into the timing of the need for a four-runway airport to cater for the growth of traffic at existing airports serving the London area, to consider the various alternative sites, and to recommend which site should be selected."[4] This body spent some two years conducting research into the matter, including lengthy public hearings. During this period, the debate grew into an emotional battle between advocates of the most economically attractive possibility and those of the most environmentally sound. It is difficult to convey the national preoccupation of Britain with these questions during this period. When it became known that the site to be chosen was likely to be the rural area around Cublington, in Buckinghamshire, there were howls of displeasure from environmentalists. For this was felt to be an exceptionally picturesque area of immense environmental significance. One member of the planning commission took such serious exception to the choice on environmental and other grounds that he declined to sign the report. He quickly became a sort of national folk hero among the generally well-educated and articulate environmentalists.

By the time the report of the commission was officially released, in December of 1970, criticism of it had already become intense. The government, by now Conservative, which received the report found a much more promising course in the recommendation of its dissenting member. That was to site the new installation at Foulness, a less populous but much more remote location, virtually at the shores of the English Channel. Although building at Foulness would be more costly and would require the development of very expensive

[4] Peter Bromhead, *The Great White Elephant of Maplin Sands* (London: Paul Elek, 1973), p. 21.

ground-transport links to London, the environmentalists insisted that the price was worth paying. When the government announced its choice of Foulness over Cublington in 1971, the sense of relief was almost palpable. The only dark spots in the picture, apparently, were nagging concerns about the economic disadvantages of Foulness and worry over the previously unnoticed aesthetic and environmental significance of the new site.

Imagine, then, the chagrin when a year or so later planners and politicians announced another turn in their thinking: The third London airport apparently would not be necessary. More efficient scheduling of landings and departures, greater reliance on new kinds of aircraft, and slowed growth of air travel would conspire to keep needs within existing capacity. Moreover, it appeared, the information on which these conclusions were based had been available throughout the most intense public debate over the issue. But the mind-set established by the planning context had proved too formidable to admit consideration of this vastly simplifying possibility.

It is too easy to snicker at the ironies in this chain of events; who, after all, can claim immunity to these forces? The remarkable thing is how thoroughly the critical faculties of many very thoughtful people were structured by the official alternatives. For months and years people debated the siting of the third London airport; yet practically no one seemed to realize that the most important choices had been ruled out of discussion. One cannot help but wonder how many such choices one accepts unreflectively under the intellectual constraints imposed by public planning.

Thus it has been, we feel, in the response to the privacy issue. People have reflexively concluded that, because more efficient and relentless personal-data management is possible, that it is to that extent desirable and even inevitable. As one spokesman for planners of electronic funds-transfer system put it,

> EFTS is happening because it is a better way. All arguments about the sufficiency of the present paper system are meaningless. Television did not come about because the radio system was overloaded or breaking down, nor did radio or the telephone develop because the mail was about to collapse. Neither were these systems built be-

> cause the public was crying for their development. They came about simply because they represented a "better way" of communication.[5]

But the obvious question is, What does "better" mean in an argument like this one, and what range of alternatives have been taken into account in making the implied comparison? Often "better" may mean nothing more than more of the same—more efficiency, more speed, more information, or more power to particular interests—with no examination of the longer-term ends thus served.

[5] R. H. Long, "EFT Systems, Banking, and Regulation J: A Report by the ACT Division of BAI," Park Ridge, Ill., Bank Administration Institute, 1974; quoted in Rob Kling, "Value Conflicts and Social Choice in Electronic Funds Transfer System Developments," *Communications of the Association for Computing Machinery,* Vol. 21, No. 8, August 1978.

22 □ Rational Planning and the Growth of Human Control

The pitfalls of rational planning are not new. Exclusion of important but disturbing alternatives, prejudice in categorizing conditions as fixed or variable—these things are as old as people's attempt to make sense of their world and plan accordingly. Indeed, such lapses are as much a part of everyday thought as they are of collective planning efforts. But the conditions of planning in modern, highly developed societies make vigilance against these shortcomings increasingly important. As the power of human beings to reshape their world grows, so, too, grows the scale of disaster when plans fail, or when this power is turned against other humans. The issues raised by surveillance thus exemplify a much broader category of characteristically modern planning dilemmas.

Evolutionary-minded social theorists have often characterized the course of social change as entailing progressive enhancement of human *control*. The notion of control has been interpreted in several different ways. A number of anthropologists, for example, have treated evolution in terms of human control over natural energy forms.[1] Thus they contrast the

[1] See Leslie A. White, "Energy and the Evolution of Culture," in *The Science of Culture: A Study of Man and Civilization* (New York: Farrar, Straus, 1949).

modest energy uses of our early hunting and gathering progenitors—say, in campfires—with the enormous amounts of natural energy captured in modern, complex societies through the use of such things as fossil fuels, hydroelectric power, and the like. The growth of larger and more complex societies, they note, typically both requires and gives rise to higher natural energy consumption per capita.

Yet another form of human control which grows with the development of larger and more complex social structures is control over those structures themselves. The exercise of power plays a role in all social relationships, from the family and the tribe to the corporation and nation-state. But the growth of larger social structures inevitably means growth in the ability of relative handfuls of actors to make and enforce binding decisions. Political leaders in a tribe exercise less power than those in a confederation or a nation-state; one might say the same for key figures in economic, legal, or religious institutions. The larger the social structures, the more power of various kinds there is, and such power is never altogether evenly distributed. The use of such power need not be oppressive; it may be exercised through processes which run from democratic to absolutist. But the coordination of human affairs within large social units always entails some concentration of binding authority over human lives.

Thus we might view very modern, highly "developed" social systems as characterized by reliance on especially powerful technologies. These include technologies of natural-energy use, as everyone knows these days. But modern social systems also have developed what one might call powerful social technologies—techniques for mobilizing the efforts of large numbers of people in concerted action. These techniques afford relative handfuls of decision-makers the means, for example, to activate party faithful in politics; or to direct the movement of investment capital; or to orchestrate the movement of armies in military campaigns; or to determine what people will read or hear or see via mass communications. Surveillance systems, of course, represent simply another refinement in social technologies. They enable elites to monitor the individual behavior of very many persons at a time, and to use the data so acquired to shape social behavior in return.

The growth of what we have called powerful technologies—surveillance very much included here—raises the *stakes* of social planning. When the technologies of small-scale, simple social systems go wrong, the numbers of persons to be affected will at least not be too great. But when the powerful technologies of large-scale, modern societies meet with destructive uses, the results may take the form of nuclear warfare or totalitarianism. Individually, there may not be a great deal to choose between victimization in a witch hunt in a seventeenth-century New England small town and persecution in a modern totalitarian regime. But collectively, the scope of human tragedy in the second case must surely be counted far greater.

The dawning realization of the potential evils of powerful technologies gone wrong has injected into contemporary culture a deep ambivalence about science and its status in society. Throughout most of the nineteenth century, the idea grew that enhanced scientific understanding of both the natural and social worlds would lead to a richer, more materially bountiful and less socially conflict-ridden existence for everyone. "Know, in order to foretell; foretell, in order to control"—thus one might translate Comte's optimistic dictum on the spirit of science. Certainly the growth both of scientific understanding and of the resulting scope of human control shows that we have followed Comte's advice. But the expanding sphere of human control has been a mixed blessing. For members of advanced, affluent societies, life has become more comfortable in countless ways. Yet the unintended effects of the technologies which afford such affluence give rise to the possibility of all sorts of man-made disasters on a scale never before possible. The use in warfare of sophisticated technologies for mobilizing energy for the first time raises the possibility of the extinction of the species. The applications of other sophisticated natural-science technologies raises serious possibilities of environmental disaster. And the growth of social technologies, including but not limited to surveillance, raises the possibility of totalitarianism. The growth of human control offers the drawbacks of its successes.

These realizations cast an ironic light on the original, almost unbounded optimism concerning the social effects of science, an optimism which social science has until very recently helped to promote.[2] In many of that earlier evolutionary interpretations of social development, the enhancement of human control was seen as a virtually unambiguous gain in the *security* of social life. After all, the growth of more powerful technologies promised to preserve human life from the uncertainties of disease, scarcity, and superstition. These "uncertainty-reducing" features of social organization thus seemed to offer a more secure role of humankind on the planet. A number of social scientists have contended, even very recently, that growing understanding of social processes will make social systems "more rational." But now we must face the fact that modern natural technologies have created highly *un*steady states. Though we may live in many ways a more bountiful material life, say, than the indigenous North American peoples, we know that present patterns of technology and energy use, drawing as they do on limited natural resources, cannot continue indefinitely. Thus our relations with our natural environments are *less* stable over the longer run than those of less "developed" peoples.[3] Similarly, the development of surveillance and the countless other sophisticated social arrangements of bureaucratic civilization offer all sorts of enriching comforts and conveniences. But no one can be certain when we may come to regret the long-term effects of the application of such powerful systems.

As the powers of powerful technologies grow more and more sweeping, the consequences of their misuse obviously become more grave. Under these conditions, the limitations of vision reflected in what has been called "the ideology of planning" take on special importance. What ought to be subjected to especially searching criticism is the unquestioning assumption that the extension of powerful technologies necessarily represents a victory for "progress" or "rationality." This is the incremental thinking which moves from the assumption that purposive control of the environment is good,

[2] The durability of such reflexive optimism in the face of all sorts of danger signs is truly remarkable. See, for example, Ithiel de Sola Pool, Stuart McIntosh, and David Griffel, "Information Systems and Social Knowledge," in Alan F. Westin, ed., *Information Technology in a Democracy* (Cambridge, Mass.: Harvard University Press, 1971).

[3] For a penetrating exploration of the weaknesses of evolutionary arguments, see Mark Granovetter, "The Idea of 'Advancement' in Theories of Social Evolution and Development," *American Journal of Sociology*, Vol. 85, No. 3, November 1979.

to the conclusion that unlimited amounts of it are always better. Such thinking discourages consideration of a key line of alternatives. These are the possibilities that some forms of human control—over both the natural and the social worlds—may be so sweeping that their development is better untried.

There are many pertinent examples. Meteorologists have recently raised the possibility that extension of knowledge in their fields might well afford a technology of weather control. Clearly the extension of control over this classical area of uncertainty would offer all sorts of benefits in agriculture, transport, recreation, and other areas. But no less obviously, such an enhancement of human powers would also extend the scope of social conflicts, and the possibility of man-made disaster. Do we really wish to add meteorological warfare to our current list of options for military action—already including nuclear, chemical, biological, and conventional options? For that matter, are we prepared to see our domestic politics enlivened by disputes over such matters as whether Northern California's annual appropriation of sunny afternoons has been interfering with precipitation subsidies for spring planting in the Midwest? Are we prepared to deal with the *politicization* of weather and climate bound to arise, should they be subjected to effective control? Or would a more rational and prudent course of action be to leave this particular form of control untried?

The dangers associated with very powerful technologies are of several different kinds. The most straightforward of these is the danger of deliberate destructive use of the powers conferred by such technologies. A second kind of danger, in the case of many natural-science technologies, is that techniques used for unexceptionable purposes may prove, later on, to entail previously unknown, destructive side effects. The effects of aerosols on the atmosphere and of certain drugs upon unborn children are some of the best-known examples here. Finally, some forms of manipulation of the natural world seem so fundamental and potentially sweeping in their effects that mere experimentation with them may hold dangers even for persons quite unassociated with the experiments. Some well-qualified researchers have taken this attitude toward experimentation with DNA. The possibility that new life forms developed in the course of these experiments might prove unprecedentedly destructive to all human life was for a time taken seriously enough to result in the sharp restriction of this research. At the time of this writing, such concerns seem to be ebbing. But given that the researches involved are inherently unprecedented, and that the resulting side effects could be utterly unacceptable, extraordinary caution is surely warranted.

To be sure, many anticipations of the potential damage brought about by extensions of human control have proved, in hindsight, to be unrealistic. At the time of construction of the Panama Canal, we are told, some British observers feared that the completed work would release the Gulf Stream into the Pacific, thus creating arctic climates in Britain and elsewhere in Northern Europe. Perhaps discussion among the best-informed minds at the time could have discounted this possibility; perhaps not. But again, the application of new technologies always entails trying something at least slightly unprecedented for the first time. The fact that a given concern seems ridiculous in retrospect need not mean that the original conception of that concern, given available evidence, was necessarily faulty.

What sharpens these concerns, at least in the case of natural-science technologies, is what one might call the increasingly fundamental nature of human intervention. Something about the growing sophistication of modern science seems to make even very circumscribed explorations of new forms of human control potentially dangerous. In the case of DNA research, some very thoughful observers felt that unanticipated results of experimentation even within a single laboratory might hold life-threatening consequences for the entire human race. Similar concerns attach to the possibilities of far-reaching consequences from accidents in chemical and bacteriological warfare preparations. The forces being tapped are so fundamental that a single mistake can, in principle, be extremely costly.

In the case of surveillance, we note no such sweeping dangers associated with experimentation on a small scale. But the risks of large-scale harnessing of these social technologies parallel those of implementing powerful natural technologies. Like nuclear-power generation and creation of new genetic materials through DNA research, the development of sophisticated mass surveillance and social control puts immense power in the hands of a few. Like other sophisticated technologies, these offer enormous benefits when used for constructive ends. But when very sophisticated technologies go wrong, the consequences may be extraordinarily unacceptable—so much so that the possibility of avoiding such technologies altogether, or of systematically limiting certain of their applications, must be taken seriously as one of the options for rational planning.

Whether dangers arising from the use of new technologies can be known and assessed adequately in advance promises to be a point on which all sorts of important public debates will turn. The classical instances in recent years have been conflicts over DNA experimentation and nuclear-power generation. Technological optimists have held that the risks entailed in these activities can indeed be known in advance, known thoroughly enough to warrant confidence that they lie within "acceptable" limits. The technological skeptics dispute such arguments on at least two grounds. First, they often hold that the optimists' assessment of identifiable risks is simply too low. Second, and more subtly, the skeptics maintain that certain risks cannot be assessed in advance. Thus these debates come to turn on highly charged questions of whether particular forms of risk assessment really touch on the essential nature of the risks at stake in implementing the new technology—and on whether the powers of human reason are strong enough to ensure control over technologies which are both novel and potentially extremely destructive.

In the planning of surveillance, the problem is not so much that the risks raised by the systems are qualitatively mysterious. Rather it is that people dispute the likelihood of risks whose nature can be understood, or the desirability of the effects in question. People may agree as to what constitute excessive or destructive applications of social power through surveillance systems; they may understand the principle of the chilling effects of efficient surveillance. Yet they may still disagree over how real such dangers are. Are they immediate, concrete risks, sufficiently serious to warrant sacrifice to forestall them? Or are they remote and farfetched, comparable to other very distant risks which we accept every day? Were the misuses of federal surveillance capabilities in the Nixon years uncharacteristic anomalies in American life unlikely to be repeated in the foreseeable future? Or were they events which can be expected to occur whenever those in power sense themselves in extreme political danger? Did they represent the most extreme possible misuse of surveillance powers of such agencies as the FBI and the IRS? Or were these effects of changing political climates likely to seem mild by comparison to others to follow?

Obviously we belong among those skeptical about the acceptability of risks associated with very powerful technologies. This attitude does not demand categorical rejection of all such technologies, but rather especially rigorous scrutiny of the potential costs of such technologies. Endless growth in the power and scope of human technologies must not be regarded as a fixed condition of modern social life. Instead, we must view the rise of human powers of control as something which may be altered if thoughtful planning so dictates. And the more sweeping those powers of control, the greater the destruction to result if they should go wrong, the deeper one's skepticism must be. Thus we oppose the view that risks of damage on a small scale are as acceptable as the risks of the same forms of damage on a more sweeping scale. Quantitative change in the scope of human powers must bring qualitative change in attitude toward the risks which they entail.

The refusal to confront these issues in any systematic way has been the most flagrant shortcoming of official discussions of privacy policy. Indeed, many of the official writings and pronouncements on the subject read as though designed to distract attention from these issues—though we doubt that this was ever anyone's conscious intent. One of the relatively rare exceptions is a brief mention by Frits Hondius, in his book *Emerging Data Protection in Europe*.[4] The development of centralized practices for monitoring people's lives, he argues, warrants no *special* concern, since it represents only one of many centralizing tendencies in modern societies. Centralized systems of transport and communication, for example, also raise some risk of repressive application of centralized power. But, Hondius implies, we do not consider returning to a feudal system of local autonomies in transport and communications simply in order to forestall centralized despotism. There is no greater reason, then, to arrest the natural development of centralized surveillance.

[4] Frits W. Hondius, *Emerging Data Protection in Europe* (New York: American Elsevier, 1975), p. 235.

Hondius dismisses the issue so briefly that one doubts that he considers it very serious. But his observations certainly warrant consideration. Obviously we have not considered the curtailment of centralized institutions or scientific thinking *in general* as promising ways of forestalling the undesirable effects of these systems. But surveillance technologies play nowhere near so indispensable a part in our lives as do these things. For many, perhaps most, powerful surveillance systems, one can imagine less information-intensive alternatives which do not lend themselves nearly so readily to centralized social control. For loosening the rigor of modern surveillance, we need not pay a dear price in any key social values. We need not seriously threaten our level of material comfort, for example, or sacrifice the values of a diverse and vigorous cultural or political life. In short, the costs of curtailing the growth of surveillance capabilities do not amount to a return to a feudal world of isolated local autonomies. And eliminating the drawbacks of these systems surely is worth the price to be paid in reduced bureaucratic efficiency here and there.

Ten years ago these arguments probably would have struck nearly everyone as hopelessly utopian. Today, perhaps, this is slightly less the case. We have lately been witnessing, in America and other highly developed societies, a profound disenchantment with powerful technologies, at least as they relate to the nonhuman world. These attitudes are perhaps most evident with regard to environmental and energy policy. As everyone knows who has been attentive to public debates on these matters, there is considerable antagonism toward powerful, centralized approaches to these issues. These are of course the same people who prefer "soft" energy technologies such as wind and water power, technologies which disperse both social and natural power into as many relatively autonomous elements as possible.

In our view, some elements of radical environmentalism have their own irrational tinge. But many of the concerns of the technological skeptics embody certain unassailably valid principles. Very powerful technologies—both social and natural—entail the risks of putting all of one's eggs in a single basket; any disaster is apt to be a very large-scale disaster indeed. By contrast, the failures of "soft," dispersed technologies at least limit the scope of the resulting damage. No one who thinks carefully about it can really like the idea of a world in which man-made concentrations of power grow larger endlessly. Yet only self-conscious efforts to enlarge the array of alternatives considered in planning for these things can reverse the trend in this direction.

If we are right, the current erosion of faith in the prospects of growing human control represents a trend of major significance. People are growing skeptical of more and more powerful technologies as solutions to the problems of highly developed societies. These changes in public attitudes cry out for a redefinition of rationality in these respects. Thoughtful, scientifically reputable people must be prepared to affirm that preference for smaller, more modest forms of control need not be superstitious or irrational. People need to hear it said that limitations on the scope of human intervention need not be antiscientific, but may simply reflect the humility required in planning for situations in which the stakes may grow very great indeed. In short, we need a program for rational limits to the extension of "rational" human control.

Happily, a number of thoughtful commentators have begun to develop such a position. Regarding the risks of nuclear power production, for example, Amitai Etzioni has written,

> To say that reactors have a 1 out of 10,000 chance to blow each year (or 1 out of 1,000,000 per community), which makes them about as safe as flying, does not take into account the number of persons to be killed in a nuclear disaster. . . . Most persons who would accept a $10.00 bet at odds of 99 to 1 in their favor, would hesitate if the bet was $1000 at the *same* odds, and refuse a $100,000 bet at *identical* odds. Why? Only because the disutility had changed.[5]

Moreover, as Etzioni would undoubtedly also emphasize, calculations regarding nuclear power must be calculations of *cumulative* probability. That is, one's concern must be with the probability of such systems' *ever* going seriously wrong; these probabilities of course rise steadily over the time span under consideration. And we hold that planning for powerful technologies in general, either natural or social, must rely on this form of thinking. One wishes to be as certain as possible

[5] Letter to the Editor, *New York Times Magazine*, 24 March 1974.

that a surveillance system *never* becomes a vehicle for repressive control. Such assurances are difficult to come by in changing political and social climates.

In another context, Kenneth Boulding has written,

> One of the major principles of the universe as a general system is that over a long enough period of time very improbable events will have happened. It is easy to show that an event with a probability of 1/n in a year has a probability of happening equal to .9995 at some time in a period of 10n years. Thus, a 100–year flood is virtually certain to happen sometime within 1000 years. Within the ten billion-year history of the universe it is virtually certain that some event with a probability of one billionth per annum will have come off.[6]

Of course, it is comforting to assume that events which we regard as unlikely are really such remote possibilities as to be discountable. But Boulding's observation should remind us of the cumulative increase of unwanted risks over time. In developing social and technological powers which have the potential of shaping both our own world and that of succeeding generations, prudence in dealing with risks of very serious occurrences is surely warranted.

The stunning development of modern surveillance has left us to cope with the embarrassments of success. Modern planners confront a social world made disorderly by the multiplicities of human biographies, characteristics, abilities, and intentions. The utterly understandable desire to predict, monitor, and control these sources of disorder has fostered increasingly sophisticated techniques. Now large organizations can know more and more pertinent things about the people with whom they deal, and act more efficiently to master the uncertainties posed in those dealings. But no conscientious thinker can help but wonder whether these successes may not be taking us too far. In monitoring more and more areas of human life, surveillance systems threaten to rob us of some of the deepest inherent satisfactions of aloneness and privacy. In

[6] "The Universe as a General System. Fourth Annual Ludwig von Bertalanffy Memorial Lecture," *Behavioral Science*, Vol. 22, No. 4, July 1977, p. 301.

recording people's past misdeeds and shortcomings, they may erode a desirable element of "forgetfulness" in social relations. And in developing sweeping capacities to monitor and shape wider and wider areas of more and more lives, they may accrue potentials for manipulation which are better off left untried. Like other powerful modern technologies, the social technologies of surveillance threaten to work too well.

The drawbacks of developing these capabilities might be worth accepting if more compelling social goods were at stake. If systems like these were the only things standing between members of modern societies and acute material want, or anarchy of the sort feared by Hobbes, or curtailment of reasoned debate over public affairs, or some other truly indispensable social value, then matters would be much different. But this is not the case. Under some circumstances the growth of surveillance may assure increments of efficiency and cost savings, but these are hardly preeminent needs of modern societies. What our societies may be in danger of losing, however, are desirable qualities of looseness and distance between central powers and individuals. These qualities, we think, help protect freedom and foster a priceless sense of diversity and autonomy. Surely a modest sacrifice of efficiency on their behalf is worth the cost to a civilized people.

Appendix

SOME MAJOR CONGRESSIONAL HEARINGS AND REPORTS RELATED TO THE PRIVACY ISSUE, 1965–77

Item/Date	*Committee*	*Topic*
Hearings 2/65–9/66	Senate, Committee on the Judiciary, Subcommittee on Administrative Practice and Procedure	Investigation of Federal and private use of electronic surveillance, Post Office surveillance of the mails, and Post Office surveillance of its employees
Hearings 6/65	Senate, Committee on the Judiciary, Subcommittee on Constitutional Rights	Examination of use of psychological tests by the federal government
Hearings 6/65–5/66	House, Committee on Government Operations, Special Subcommittee on Invasion of Privacy	Federal use of personality tests and the Department of Agriculture's Farm Census
Hearings 7/66	House, Committee on Government Operations, Special Subcommittee on Invasion of Privacy	First hearings on the National Data Center

Item/Date	*Committee*	*Topic*
Hearings 9–10/66	Senate, Committee on the Judiciary Subcommittee on Constitutional Rights	Consideration of a bill, introduced by Senator Ervin, to protect the constitutional rights of government employees and prohibit unwarranted invasions of their privacy. Polygraph screenings, psychological testing, security clearances, and improper investigative practices were among the topics covered
Report 1966	Senate, Committee on the Judiciary Subcommittee on Constitutional Rights	Reviewed subcommittee hearings on psychological testing in the federal government
Hearings 3/67	Senate, Committee on the Judiciary, Subcommittee on Administrative Practice and Procedure	Consideration of the establishment of a National Data Center
Hearings 3-5/67	Senate, Committee on the Judiciary, Subcommittee on Administrative Practice and Procedure	The Right of Privacy Act of 1967, a bill to restrict wiretapping, submitted by the Johnson Administration. This bill did not reach a floor vote in the Senate.
Hearings 5-6/67	Congress, Joint Economic Committee, Subcommittee on Economic Statistics	Coordination of Federal statistics; Heard testimony in favor of the National Data Center

Item/Date	*Committee*	*Topic*
Report 1967	Senate, Committee on the Judiciary Subcommittee on Administrative Practice and Procedure	A survey of information on individuals maintained by federal agencies
Report 8/68	Senate, Committee on the Judiciary, Subcommittee on Constitutional Rights	Report accompanying a Senate bill to protect the privacy of federal employees
Hearings 3/68	House, Committee on Government Operations	Information practices of the commercial credit reporting industry; increasing centralization within the industry; the impact of the computer on industry practices
Hearings 5/68	House, Committee on Government Operations.	Investigation of the personal-record practices of the Retail Credit Co. (now Equifax)
Hearings 4–7/69	Senate, Committee on the Judiciary, Subcommittee on Constitutional Rights	Constitutional propriety of questions asked of citizens on census forms and federal questionnaires
Hearings 4–5/69	Congress, Joint Economic Committee, Subcommittee on Economic Statistics	Examination of whether certain questions in 1970 census constitute unwarranted invasion of privacy
Hearings 5/69	Senate, Committee on Banking and Currency, Subcommittee on Financial Institutions	Examination of need for legislation to regulate some information practices of the credit industry

Item/Date	*Committee*	*Topic*
Hearings 5/69	House, Committee on Post Office and Civil Service, Subcommittee on Census and Statistics	Assessment of needs of local communities for census data; public responses to requirements of 1970 census were sampled
Hearings 4–6/69	House, Committee on Post Office and Civil Service, Subcommittee on Census and Statistics	Review of mandatory requirement questions included in the decennial census
Report 1969	House, Committee on Post Office and Civil Service	Materials concerning a bill to strengthen confidentiality and eliminate the jail-sentence penalty for refusal to cooperate with census requirements
Report 1969	Senate, Committee on Banking and Currency	Review of proposals which would enable consumers to protect themselves against arbitrary, erroneous, and malicious credit information
Hearings 3–4/70	House, Committee on Banking and Currency, Subcommittee on Consumer Affairs	Testimony on the necessity of legislation to protect the civil rights of credit customers
Report 1970	Senate, Committee on Judiciary, Subcommittee on Constitutional Rights	Summary of issues pertaining to constitutional rights from 2/1/67 to 1/31/70—rights of federal employees, census questions, and federal data banks

Item/Date	*Committee*	*Topic*
Report 1970	Senate, Committee on the Judiciary	Review of proposals to protect the employees of the executive branch of the U.S. Government in the enjoyment of their constitutional rights and to prevent unwarranted government invasion of their privacy
Report 1970	House, Committee on Science and Astronautics	Privacy problems in the computer age. Recommended Executive Agency and Congressional committees to provide research and regulation
Hearings 2–3/71	Senate, Committee on the Judiciary, Subcommittee on Constitutional Rights	Military surveillance of civilians, and computerized government data banks
Hearings 5–6/71	House, Committee on Post Office and Civil Service. Subcommittee on Employee Benefits	Privacy problems of federal employees, with a view toward proposing corrective legislation
Report 1971	House, Committee on Post Office and Civil Service	Recommendation of guarantees against disclosure of census information and removal of jail sentence penalty for refusal to answer mandatory inquiries
Report 1971	Senate, Committee on the Judiciary	Protecting Privacy and the Rights of Federal Employees

Item/Date	*Committee*	*Topic*
Hearings 3–4/72	House, Committee on the Judiciary, Subcommittee on Security and Privacy of Criminal Arrest Records	Exploration of methods of safeguarding, simultaneously, individual privacy and the needs of law-enforcement officials
Hearings 3–5/72	House, Committee on Interstate and Foreign Commerce, Special Subcommittee on Investigations	Review of why an employee of the Federal Communications Commission was subjected to telephone surveillance in February 1970
Hearings 6/72	House, Committee on Government Operations, Subcommittee on Foreign Operations and Government Information	Records maintained by government agencies
Hearings 8/72	Senate, Committee on Banking, Housing and Urban Affairs	Examination of legislation to amend the Bank Secrecy Act, to restrict access to private bank accounts
Report 1972	Senate, Committee on Judiciary (in conjunction with the Civil Rights Commission)	Recommendation of a bill to protect the constitutional rights and privacy of federal employees
Hearings 4/73	House, Committee on Post Office and Civil Service, Subcommittee on Census and Statistics	Confidentiality of information in response to questionnaires, inquiries, and other requests of the Bureau of Census
Hearings 4–7/73	House, Committee on Government Operations, Foreign Oper-	Examination of infromation and communications

Item/Date	*Committee*	*Topic*
	ations and Government Information Subcommittee	system employed by various federal agencies
Hearings 5–8/73	House, Committee on Government Operations, Foreign Operations and Government Information Subcommittee	Investigation of an executive order authorizing the Department of Agriculture to obtain certain private information from the income-tax returns of farmers
Hearings 1973	Senate, Committee on Banking, Housing and Urban Affairs, Subcommittee on Consumer Credit	The Fair Credit Reporting Act of 1973
Report 1973	House, Committee on Interstate and Foreign Committee on Interstate and Foreign Commerce, Special Subcommittee on Investigations	Complete report on a 1970 wiretap incident at the Federal Communications Commission
Hearings 2–5/74	House, Committee on Government Operations, Subcommittee on Foreign Operations and Government Information	Access to federal records
Hearings 3/74	Senate, Committee on the Judiciary, Subcommittee on Constitutional Rights	Criminal Justice Data Banks
Hearings 4–5/74	Senate, Joint Hearings before the Administrative Practice and Procedure Subcommittee	Wiretapping and electronic surveillance

Item/Date	*Committee*	*Topic*
	and Constitutional Rights Subcommittee (Judiciary committee) and the Subcommittee on Surveillance (Foreign Relations Committee)	
Hearings 6/74	Senate, Government Operations Committee, Ad Hoc Subcommittee on Privacy and Information Systems; Committee on the Judiciary, Subcommittee on Constitutional Rights	Privacy and the collection, use, and computerization of personal data
Hearings 6/74	House, Committee on Government Operations, Subcommittee on Government Information and Individual Rights	Telephone monitoring by federal agencies
Hearings 7/74	Senate, Committee on Banking, Housing and Urban Affairs, Subcommittee on Financial Institutions	The effect of the Bank Secrecy Act on state laws
Hearings 1974	House, Committee on the Judiciary	Dissemination of Criminal Justice Information
Report 1974	Senate, Committee on Government Operations	Protecting individual privacy in federal gathering, Use and Disclosure of Information
Report 1974	Senate, Committee on the Judiciary	Protecting the privacy and rights of federal employees

Item/Date	*Committee*	*Topic*
Hearings 4/75	Senate, Committee on Finance, Subcommittee on Administration of the IRS Code	Consideration of legislation to regulate the use and disclosure of Internal Revenue Service tax records. None of the proposed bills was enacted; instead less stringent provisions were incorporated into Tax Reform Act of 1976
Hearings 5–11/75	House, Committee on Post Office and Civil Service, Subcommittee on Postal Facilities, Mail and Labor Management	Abuses of the mails by federal agencies
Hearings 6/75	House, Committee on Government Operations, Subcommittee, Special Subcommittee on Invasion of Privacy	Investigation of the progress of federal agencies in implementing the Privacy Act of 1974
Hearings 7/75	Senate, Committee on the Judiciary, Subcommittee on Constitutional Rights	Examination of proposed legislation (Criminal Justice Information and Protection of Privacy Act) to restrict the use and disclosure of types of arrest and criminal history information
Hearings 9–12/75	Senate, Select Committee to Study Government Operations	Nixon administration plans for domestic surveillance; Internal Revenue Service abuses; mail opening; national security and Fourth Amendment rights; Federal Bureau of Investigation abuses

Item/Date	*Committee*	*Topic*
Hearings 10–11/75	Senate, Committee on Banking, Housing and Urban Affairs, Subcommittee on Consumer Affairs	Fair Credit Reporting Act Amendments of 1975
Hearings 1975	House, Committee on Government Operations	Examination of CIA exemptions from the Privacy Act of 1974
Report 1975	Senate, Committee on Government Operations	Protection of personal information in Europe
Hearings 1/76	House, Committee on Ways and Means	Confidentiality of tax information gathered by the Internal Revenue Service; sharing of IRS data with other agencies
Hearings 1–4/76	Senate, Committee on Finance, Subcommittee on Administration of the Internal Revenue Code	Collection, use, and disclosure of tax-return and tax-related information
Hearings 6/76	Senate, Committee on Banking, Housing and Urban Affairs, Subcommittee on Financial Institutions	Examination of the Right to Financial Privacy Act, which would place restrictions on government access to individual financial transaction records
Report 1976	Congress, Senate Committee on Government Operations; House, Committee on Government Operations	Legislative history of the Privacy Act of 1974

Date/Item	*Committee*	*Topic*
Hearings 1977	Senate, Government Operations Committee	Consideration of a one-year extension of the Privacy Protection Study Commission

Source: Congressional Record.

Bibliography

This is not an exhaustive bibliography. Included here are only sources which have been of direct use to us in preparing this work. The most complete bibliography on the subject known to us is that kept by the Information Privacy Research Center at Purdue University; it consisted of some 2,500 items as of early 1979.

Adams, Richard. *Energy and Structure: A Theory of Social Power.* Austin: University of Texas Press, 1975.

American Federation of Information Processing Societies, *A National Survey of the Public's Attitudes Toward Computers.* New York: Time, Inc., n.d.

Askin, Frank. "Surveillance: The Social Science Perspective," *Columbia Human Rights Law Review,* Vol. 4, No. 1 (Winter 1972).

Baker, Michael A. "Record Privacy as a Marginal Problem: The Limits of Consciousness and Concern," *Columbia Human Rights Law Review,* Vol. 4, No. 1 (Winter 1972).

Bates, Alan. "Privacy—A Useful Concept?" *Social Forces,* Vol. 42, No. 4 (May 1964).

Baxter, William F., Paul H. Cootner and Kenneth E. Scott, *Retail Banking in the Electronic Age.* Montclair, N.J.: Allanheld, Osmun, 1977.

Boguslaw, Robert. *The New Utopians.* Englewood Cliffs, N.J.: Prentice-Hall, 1965.

Boulding, Kenneth. "The Universe as a General System. Fourth

Annual Ludwig von Bertalanffy Memorial Lecture," *Behavioral Science*, Vol. 22, No. 4 (July 1977).

Brenton, Myron. *The Privacy Invaders.* New York: Coward-McCann, 1964.

Bromhead, Peter. *The Great White Elephant of Maplin Sands.* London: Paul Elek, 1973.

Burnham, David. "The Watch on Computer Privacy," *New York Times,* 15 January 1978.

———, "FBI Data Network Poses Privacy Issue," *New York Times,* 17 July 1978.

Bushkin, Arthur A., and Samuel I. Schaen. *The Privacy Act of 1974: A Reference Manual for Compliance.* McLean, Va.: System Development Corporation, 1976.

Canada. *Privacy and Computers.* A report of a Task Force established jointly by Department of Communications/Department of Justice Ottawa, Information Canada, 1972.

Carneiro, Robert L., ed. *The Evolution of Society: Selections from Herbert Spencer's Principles of Sociology.* Chicago: University of Chicago Press, 1967.

Central Intelligence Agency. *Where's What: Sources of Information for Federal Investigators.* New York: Quadrangle/New York Times Book Co., n.d.

Chandler, Alfred, Jr. *The Visible Hand: The Managerial Revolution in American Business.* Cambridge, Mass.: Belknap/Harvard University Press, 1977.

Chommie, John C. *The Internal Revenue Service.* New York: Praeger, 1970.

Commission Informatique et Libertés. *Rapport.* Paris: La Documentation Française, 1975.

Congressional Quarterly, *Almanac. 92nd Congress. 1st Session, 1971.* Washington, D.C.: Congressional Quarterly, 1972.

Coser, Lewis A. *Masters of Sociological Thought.* New York: Harcourt Brace Jovanovich, 1977.

Dalentius, Tore and Anders Klevmarken. *Proceedings* of a Symposium on Personal Integrity and the Need for Data in the Social Sciences, held at Hässelby Slott, Stockholm, March 15–17, 1976. Swedish Council for Social Science Research, n.d.

Domestic Council Committee on the Right to Privacy. *National Information Policy: Report to the President of the United States.* Washington, D.C.: U.S. Government Printing Office, 1976.

Ellul, Jacques. *The Technological Society.* New York: Knopf, 1964.

Flaherty, David H. *Privacy in Colonial New England.* Charlottesville: University of Virginia Press, 1972.

Fried, Charles. "Privacy," *Yale Law Journal,* Vol. 77 (January 1968).

Friedman, Lawrence M. "Social Welfare Legislation: An Introduction," *Stanford Law Review*, Vol. 21 (January 1969).

Gallouedec-Genuys, Françoise and Herbert Maisl. *Le Secret des Fichiers*. Paris: Editions Cujas, 1976.

Godkin, E.L. "The Rights of the Citizen.—IV.—To His Own Reputation," *Scribner's*, Vol. 8 (July 1890).

Granovetter, Mark. "The Idea of 'Advancement' in Theories of Social Evolution and Development," *American Journal of Sociology*, Vol. 85, No. 3 (November 1979).

Greenawalt, Kent. *Legal Protections of Privacy*. Washington, D.C.: Office of Telecommunications Policy, 1975.

Gross, M.L. *The Brain Watchers*. New York: Signet, 1963.

Handler, Joel F. and Margaret K. Rosenheim. "Privacy in Welfare: Public Assistance and Juvenile Justice," *Law and Contemporary Problems*, Vol. 31, No. 2 (Spring 1966).

Hasenfeld, Yeheskel. "People Processing Organizations: An Exchange Approach," *American Sociological Review*, Vol. 37 (June 1972).

Hondius, Frits W. *Emerging Data Protection in Europe*. New York: American Elsevier, 1975.

Kling, Rob. "Value Conflict and Social Choice in Electronic Funds Transfer System Developments," *Communications of the Association for Computing Machinery*, Vol. 21, No. 8 (August 1978).

Laudon, Kenneth C. *Computers and Bureaucratic Reform*. New York: Wiley, 1974.

Lowi, Theodore. *The End of Liberalism*. New York: Norton, 1969.

———, *The Politics of Disorder*. New York: Basic Books, 1971.

Lowry, Ritchie. "Toward a Sociology of Secrecy and Security Systems," *Social Problems*, Vol. 19 (Spring 1972).

Mandell, Lewis. *Credit Card Use in the United States*. Ann Arbor: Institute for Social Research, University of Michigan, 1972.

Miller, Arthur R. *The Assault on Privacy*. Ann Arbor: University of Michigan Press, 1971.

Moore, Wilbert and Melvin Tumin. "Some Social Functions of Ignorance," *American Sociological Review*, Vol. 14, No. 6 (December 1949).

National Commission on Consumer Finance. *Consumer Credit in the United States* Washington, D.C.: U.S. Government Printing Office, 1972.

National Commission on Electronic Fund Transfers (sic). *EFT and the Public Interest*. Washington, D.C.: U.S. Government Printing Office, 1977.

Nevins, Allan. *Ordeal of the Union*, Vol. II. New York: Scribner, 1947.

Nizer, L. "The Right of Privacy: A Half Century's Development," *Michigan Law Review,* Vol. 39, 1941.

OECD, *Conference on Computer/Telecommunications Policy.* Proceedings of the OECD Conference February 4–6, 1975. Paris: OECD, 1976.

———. *Policy Issues in Data Protection and Privacy.* Proceedings of the OECD Conference 24th to 26th June, 1974. Paris: OECD, 1976.

Ogburn, William Fielding. *On Culture and Social Change: Selected Papers,* Otis Dudley Duncan, ed. Chicago: University of Chicago Press, 1964.

Parsons, Talcott. *Structure and Process in Modern Societies.* Glencoe, Ill.: The Free Press, 1960.

Pember, Don R. *Privacy and the Press: The Law, the Mass Media and the First Amendment.* Seattle: University of Washington Press, 1972.

Perrow, Charles. *Complex Organizations: A Critical Essay.* Glenview, Ill.: Scott Foresman and Co., 1972.

Piven, Frances Fox and Richard A. Cloward. *Regulating the Poor: The Functions of Public Welfare.* New York: Vintage Books, 1971.

Pool, Ithiel de Sola, Stuart McIntosh, and David Griffel. "Information Systems and Social Knowledge," in Alan F. Westin, ed., *Information Technology in a Democracy.* Cambridge, Mass.: Harvard University Press, 1971.

Privacy Protection Study Commission. *Personal Privacy in an Informative Society.* Washington, D.C.: U.S. Government Printing Office, 1977.

Rovere, Richard H. "The Invasion of Privacy (1): Technology and the Claims of Community," *American Scholar,* Vol. 27 (Autumn 1958).

Rule, James B. *Insight and Social Betterment; A Preface to Applied Social Science.* New York: Oxford University Press, 1978.

———. *Private Lives and Public Surveillance.* New York: Schocken, 1974.

———. *Value Choices in Electronic Funds Transfer Policy.* Washington, D.C.: Office of Telecommunications Policy, 1975.

Schwartz, Barry. "The Social Psychology of Privacy," *American Journal of Sociology,* Vol. 73 (May 1968).

Seipp, David J. *The Right to Privacy in American History.* Cambridge, Mass.: Harvard University Program on Information Resources Policy, 1978.

Shils, Edward. "Privacy and Power," in Edward Shils, *Center and Periphery: Essays in Macrosociology.* Chicago: University of Chicago Press, 1975.

Stinchcombe, Arthur L. "Institutions of Privacy in the Determination of Police Administrative Practice," *American Journal of Sociology*, Vol. 69, No. 2 (September 1963).

Stone, James. "Opinions, Findings and Decisions on 1978 Automobile Insurance Rates," Commonwealth of Massachusetts, Division of Insurance, 1977.

Thompson, James D. *Organization in Action.* New York: McGraw-Hill, 1967.

TRW Credit Data, Inc., *Press Handbook on Consumer Credit Reporting.* Long Beach, Calif.: TRW Credit Data, 1977.

U.S. Congress, *The Coordination and Integration of Government Statistical Programs.* Hearings Before the Subcommittee on Economic Statistics of the Joint Economic Committee, 90th Congress, 1st Session. Washington, D.C.: U.S. Government Printing Office, 1967.

———. *Legislative History of the Privacy Act of 1974, S. 3418 (Public Law 93–579)* Printed for the use of the Committee on Government Operations, United States Senate, and the Committee on Government Operations, House of Representatives. Washington, D.C.: U.S. Government Printing Office, 1976.

U.S. Department of Commerce, Bureau of the Census. *Historical Statistic of the United States.* Washington, D.C.: U.S. Government Printing Office, 1977.

U.S. Department of Health, Education and Welfare. Secretary's Advisory Committee on Automated Personal Data Systems. *Records, Computers and the Rights of Citizens.* Washington, D.C.: U.S. Government Printing Office, 1973.

———. *Vital Statistics of the United States.* Vol. I. Washington, D.C.: U.S. Government Printing Office, 1950.

U.S. Department of Justice. *Report of the Federal Advisory Committee on False Identification.* Washington, D.C.: U.S. Government Printing Office, 1976.

U.S. Department of State. "Summary of Passport Statistics." Passport Office, Bureau of Consular Affairs, January 1978.

U.S. Department of State. *The United States Passport: Past, Present, Future.* Washington, D.C.: U.S. Government Printing Office, 1976.

U.S. Department of the Treasury, Internal Revenue Service. *ADP in IRS.* Washington, D.C.: U.S. Government Printing Office, 1975.

———. *Integrated Data Retrieval System.* Washington D.C.: U.S. Government Printing Office, 1976.

———. *Annual Report 1977.* Washington, D.C.: U.S. Government Printing Office, 1977.

U.S. House of Representatives. *Special Inquiry on Invasions of Privacy.* Hearings before the Special Subcommittee on Invasion of Privacy of the Committee on Government Operations,

House of Representatives, 89th Congress, 1st Session. Washington, D.C.: U.S. Government Printing Office, 1965.
———. *The Computer and the Invasion of Privacy*. Hearings before the Special Subcommittee on Invasion of Privacy of the Committee on Government Operations, House of Representatives, 89th Congress, 2nd Session. Washington, D.C.: U.S. Government Printing Office, 1966.
U.S. Senate. *Invasions of Privacy*. Hearings before the Subcommittee on Administrative Practice and Procedure of the Committee of the Judiciary, United States Senate, 89th Congress, 1st Session. Washington, D.C.: U.S. Government Printing Office, 1965.
———. *Computer Privacy*. Hearings before the Subcommittee on Administrative Practice and Procedure of the Committee on the Judiciary, United States Senate, 90th Congress, 1st Session. Washington, D.C.: U.S. Government Printing Office, 1967.
———. *Federal Tax Return Privacy*. Hearings before the Subcommittee on Administration of the Internal Revenue Code of the Committee on Finance, United States Senate, 94th Congress, 2nd Session. Washington, D.C.: U.S. Government Printing Office, 1976.
Warren, Samuel, and Lewis D. Brandeis. "The Right to Privacy," *Harvard Law Review*, Vol. 4. (1890).
Weizenbaum, Joseph. *Computer Power and Human Reason*. (San Francisco: W.H. Freeman, 1976.
Wessel, Milton R. *Freedom's Edge: The Computer Threat to Society*. Reading, Mass.: Addison-Wesley, 1974.
Westin, Alan F. "Civil Liberties Issues in Public Databanks," in Alan F. Westin, ed. *Information Technology in a Democracy*. Cambridge, Mass.: Harvard University Press, 1971.
———. *Computers, Health Records, and Citizen Rights*. Sponsored by the Institute for Computer Science and Technology, National Bureau of Standards. Washington, D.C.: U.S. Government Printing Office, 1976.
———. *Privacy and Freedom*. New York: Atheneum, 1967.
Westin, Alan F. and Michael Baker. *Databanks in a Free Society*. New York: Quadrangle/New York Times Book Co., 1972.
Wheeler, Stanton, ed. *On Record: Files and Dossiers in American Life*. New York: Russell Sage Foundation, 1969.
White, Leslie A. *The Science of Culture: A Study of Man and Civilization*. New York: Farrar, Straus, 1949.
Wilensky, Harold. *Organizational Intelligence*. New York: Basic Books, 1967.
Wright, Carroll D. *The History and Growth of the United States Census*. Washington, D.C.: U.S. Government Printing Office, 1900.
Younger, Kenneth. *Report of the Committee on Privacy*. London: Her Majesty's Stationery Office, 1972.

Index

JAMES RULE is Professor of Sociology at the State University of New York, Stony Brook. His earlier book on personal-data systems, *Private Lives and Public Surveillance,* was co-recipient in 1974 of the C. Wright Mills Award of the Society for the Study of Social Problems. He is also author of *Insight and Social Betterment* (1978).

DOUGLAS MCADAM is Assistant Professor of Sociology at George Mason University in Fairfax, Virginia. His scholarly interests include social movements, gerontology, and social policy analysis. He is the author of a number of papers and articles and is at work on a book on the black protest movement in America.

LINDA STEARNS is a doctoral candidate in Sociology at the State University of New York, Stony Brook. Her research interests include urban sociology and the study of American business. Her doctoral dissertation deals with the role of investment capital in corporate decision-making.

DAVID UGLOW is a doctoral candidate in Sociology at the State University of New York, Stony Brook. His research includes studies of the social impact of personal data systems and of the relationships between bureaucracies and the public.

www.ingramcontent.com/pod-product-compliance
Lightning Source LLC
LaVergne TN
LVHW101442200926
848483LV00001B/19
9780444990747